Woodcarving
A DESIGNER'S NOTEBOOK

James E. Seitz

Sterling Publishing Co., Inc.   New York

This book is dedicated to those creative persons who have the courage to experiment with the untried, to devise new arrangements from the old, and to strive for simplicity in each endeavor.

Edited by Timothy Nolan

Library of Congress Cataloging-in-Publication Data

Seitz, James E.
    Woodcarving : a designer's notebook / James E. Seitz.
        p.   cm.
    Includes index.
    ISBN 0-8069-6978-4
    1. Wood-carving—Technique.   I. Title.
NK9704.S45   1989
736'.4—dc20   89-11427
                                                        CIP

    3   5   7   9   10   8   6   4   2

Copyright © 1989 by James E. Seitz
Published by Sterling Publishing Co., Inc.
387 Park Avenue South, New York, N.Y. 10016
Distributed in Canada by Sterling Publishing
% Canadian Manda Group, P.O. Box 920, Station U
Toronto, Ontario, Canada M8Z 5P9
Distributed in Great Britain and Euorpe by Cassell PLC
Artillery House, Artillery Row, London SW1P 1RT, England
Distributed in Australia by Capricorn Ltd.
P.O. Box 665, Lane Cove, NSW 2066
Manufactured in the United States of America
All rights reserved
Sterling ISBN 0-8069-6978-4 Paper

CONTENTS

PREFACE

Designing is an art. Were that not the case, there simply would be a list of formulas to be consulted and applied in a methodical, if not magical, way. As it is, the process gives rise to many possibilities with each shaping of an object or arrangement of a decoration. Seldom will observers totally agree on the merit and quality of results, and what is seen and enjoyed may vary even when important principles of art have been carefully applied.

Developing skill in designing does require persistence, but command of the subject is not as difficult as some experienced persons make it. Neither is it a matter of extraordinary difficulty for the beginner. A sufficiently curious person, given a guide to the basics, should be able to progress handily in the field of design. Armed with this book, a personal commitment, and a creative touch, the path towards mastery of the fundamentals could actually be smoother than anticipated.

The skilful designing of woodcarvings seems more readily caught than taught. For that reason, the text is accompanied by many photographic examples. Applications of design principles and styles are also presented for scrutiny and analysis in numerous illustrations.

In addition to developing an artistic awareness, the designer of woodcarvings must know the actual techniques of woodcarving, as well as its limitations, whether whittling, sculpturing, incising, or carving in relief. Nobody can effectively design a product without knowing the capacity of the construction process. Because of this, applying designs to the various methods of carving receives much emphasis in this book.

Whether a casual hobbyist or a devoted craftsman, the reader will find the text gives many helpful examples of how to create effective designs. The basic rules and principles are emphasized throughout, both as applied in everyday practices and in a few of ancient origin. The important design styles are also covered. These range from the realistic at one extreme to the abstract at the other. Details of how to apply the various styles and techniques will be found beneficial to woodcarvers at all levels of development.

Attention is also devoted to the craft as an art form. Consequently, methods of design are applied to decorative and to utilitarian articles, and years of experience are drawn upon to make the results specially fitting. Appropriate application, rather than elaborate detail, constitutes the main thrust of the work. The information will help practitioners learn to create effectively instead of merely using designs as given.

Credit for assisting the author must go to many people. The brevity of my comments on this matter in no way diminishes my appreciation for those mentioned, nor does it overlook the many who have contributed to my education and helped nurture a spark of creativity.

Specifically, acknowledgment is hereby given to Charles Williams for allowing use of a photograph of his naturalistically carved duck as displayed in the Pubanz Art Studio. A special word of gratitude goes to my daughter, Ellen. Her assistance with the photography is especially noteworthy. And last, my heartfelt thanks go to my wife, Arlene, and to the rest of my family for their occasional comments of support.

James E. Seitz, Ph.D.

I
THE DESIGN PROCESS

Designing is basic in woodcarving. Some thought must be directed to a subject's form at the initial point of planning and throughout every stage of development thereafter. The planning phase usually culminates in a drawing of the piece to be carved. On occasion, a craftsman will proceed with only an idea or another person's interpretation in mind. The result, in any case, depends to a large extent on the quality of the subject's design.

The practice of doing both the designing and the carving is gratifying, whether working in relief, incising, whittling, or sculpturing. Although much enjoyment may be realized by following a plan completed by another, the woodcarver who learns to create and execute designs skilfully benefits considerably. Greater personal satisfaction and recognition come to the designer-craftsman.

Typically, the beginning woodcarver must answer a question or two by close observers of his work, such as "You did all that?" and "Where did you get the idea?" The queries are often a slightly veiled attempt to give credit for having created the design. They imply that the person clever enough to have done the designing should be held in at least the same esteem as the one who did the carving. Being able to respond by taking credit for both the design and the carving instills in the craftsman a sense of otherwise unequalled accomplishment—enough, possibly, to earn consideration as an artisan.

Developing a Complete Craftsmanship

The competent woodcarver qualifies as an artisan upon learning to design skilfully. As a minimum, he must establish control of the elementary concepts of art. Balance, proportion, unity, and mass are several of the fundamentals to be mastered.

Designing skilfully, by way of explanation, does not require extraordinary artistic ability. In fact, experienced painters sometimes elicit criticism from others for depicting things from nature with astonishing accuracy and detail, while showing only limited inclination to develop anything different or new. Their art rests in representing things strictly as they are, with the able ones generally receiving credit for what they do aside from designing.

Designing flows from a creative and active imagination. Many people who do not consider themselves to be artists have the necessary creative ability. Undoubtedly, this special talent exists within a large share of the woodcarving population.

The design process embodies another intellectual requirement. It makes the use of interpretative powers essential so that results conform to accepted principles. Good results are more likely to be achieved by observing and applying the principles than by giving vent to a purely intuitive approach. The fundamentals are within the grasp of all who take time to understand and constructively use them.

Knowledge of the fundamentals becomes as important for those who copy designs as for those who create their own. To copy means first to choose. Any such selection depends on knowing the good. Whether using a selected sketch or drawing an original, the craftsman's knowledge of design will affect the quality of the finished carving as much one way as the other.

Attaining Quality

A woodcarver creates a work of quality by shaping an object according to an artistic plan, or design. Embodying principles of art in the design is a major step towards producing a carving of significance. Unless this point receives careful attention, the result may be left primarily to chance. Executing the design as intended constitutes the second important requirement.

Proficiency with tools has a profound bearing on quality, as does selecting wood according to hardness, grain, color, and size, along with the choice of protective finish. Certainly, none of these things, regardless of their inherent qualities, will compensate for an ineffective or inartistic composition. The relationships within the finished composition and the impact of the piece within its intended surroundings are all important considerations at the design stage.

Recognition as a work of art comes about as a result of both objectively analyzed elements of design and the more subjectively felt experience of beauty as judged by the observer. Understandably, differences of opinion arise. The concept of beauty varies from person to person due to divergent individual experiences, psychological and physical, and from era to era according to changing conventions. Since an observer at any point in time cannot comprehend a creation exactly as the designer conceived it, the merit of detailing. Whatever the approach used, the finishing of an object as it appears in nature requires

carved work should be based primarily on the appeal of the formal elements embodied within.

The practice of designing is fundamental to woodcarving, with few exceptions. A good design does not lead with certainty to a quality carving, but a poor one will very likely result in a deficient piece regardless of the skill with gouges and chisels on beautiful sections of wood. In that sense, the design becomes the most limiting aspect of all. Procedures for designing apply when creating any original (non-copied) work of art.

Defining Design Limits

The process of designing seems to be cautiously avoided by many woodcarvers, as can be seen in some of the displays at woodcarver's shows. Oftentimes the carvings stand out as duplicates of natural forms or close reproductions of previously drawn designs, but matters of balance, mass, and proportion receive only incidental attention in the shaping of the wood. They are taken for granted as they appear in nature or in somebody else's design.

Duplicating nature in wood in a faithful imitation is *naturalistic carving*. Illus. 1 represents objective detailing in purest form. It is a skilfully executed example of a familiar type, with much of its beauty deriving from the preciseness with which naturally occurring detail has been reproduced. Obviously, a person with a steady and careful hand produced this showpiece. It conforms as exactly to the living bird as the craftsman was able to make it.

Wildfowl carvings frequently acquire their natural appearance from the remarkable care in finishing with burning tool and paints. The wooden reproductions are sometimes made so much like the natural thing that even their added capacity to float in water at the proper depth becomes a consideration. Some observers, upon closely inspecting the details, have mistaken finished pieces for feathered fowl mounted by a taxidermist. Persons capable of producing such fine work can make a duck so lifelike that neither

Illus. 1. A replica of a female mallard showing the lifelike form and precise detail necessary in a naturalistic treatment of a woodcarving.

the largest feature nor the smallest detail are easily distinguished from those of the real thing.

Certain figures preferred by naturalists require a bare minimum of carving. Mechanically preshaped imitations of birds of nearly every kind are available, with the hobbyist having nothing more to do to finish one than apply paint after inserting manufactured eyes, legs, and beak. At times, a wooden shape will be used for which only the shafts and barbs of the feathers need be carved. Persons working the prepared shapes will often use high-speed, electrically driven cutting burrs or a burning tool for the fine as much artful control of color as it does of carving tools.

While the carving involved may be extremely limited, the amount of designing may be nil. Designing does not necessarily have a part in naturalistic representation. Composing and arranging may be altogether absent.

Every object copied as it appears in nature has prearranged features. This is important, because arranging has an essential place in design. Design finds expression through the variation of nature, while subjects carved naturalistically are, in effect, three-dimensional snapshots. Features are duplicated as viewed. Thus, naturalistic reproduction in its purest form falls outside the limits of design.

The style of execution at the other end of the spectrum is *abstraction.* Extreme forms of this style evolve idealistically and without reference to any object or to its features. Unlike imitations of nature, such abstractions derive from the idealism of the artist's imagination, and in their strictest form, flow exclusively from the imagina-

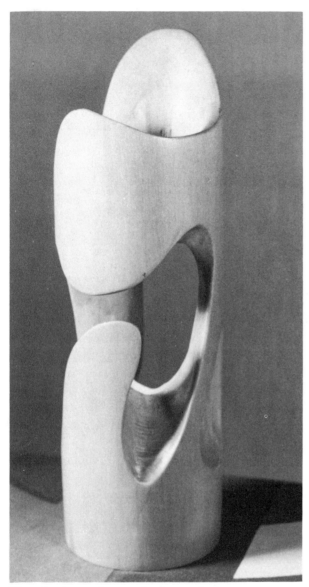

Illus. 2. A nonobjectively designed abstraction emphasizing relationships between mass and space as modified by shades of light.

Whereas the carving in Illus. 2 depicts a particular object, the sculpture in Illus. 2 does not. Only certain elements of art are brought together in an interesting arrangement.

Any beauty to be attributed to this sculpture must derive essentially from the flow of mass, the interaction of planes, and the arrangement of spatial elements. The extent to which the viewer appreciates all as intended may be a matter of personal experience. Nonobjective carving certainly has not become as widely accepted as naturalistic representation, a consequence of differences in exposure and understanding.

Neither abstraction nor naturalistic representation in their purest forms fall within the category of objective design. As a result, both continue to generate a certain amount of controversy in the field of art. Nevertheless, styles *do* occur that closely correspond to the two extremes and yet are within the range of objectively created design. Those abstract forms based on recognizable subjects and realistic arrangements of natural figures represent the limits of objective design.

Let it be said emphatically that reproducing subjects naturally, creating in isolated abstraction, or even tracing completed drawings of such designs are not in and of themselves wrong. Since the practices can lead to truly outstanding work, only the frequency of their use might be seriously questioned. Some woodcarvers seem not to accomplish all of which they are capable.

The advantages to be realized from designing as well as carving are worth the effort. Doing the design work places the woodcarver in almost total control of the craft. He becomes dreamer, director, and doer. Only the purpose of the design remains a limitation of great consequence.

Differentiating Purposes

Woodcarving designs, and hence the finished carvings, are usually made today for the purpose of creating a decorative effect. Less common are carvings for utility and the conveyance of a spiritual or symbolic meaning. The preponder-

tion and feeling of the individual. Mass, balance, texture, unity, and the like receive prominent treatment. Some proponents of this style argue that a creation should not portray a subject in any form, since the elements of artistic composition are to be captured and emphasized above all else.

This purely idealistic approach to abstraction places it in the nonobjective realm of design. A nonobjective carving is shown in Illus. 2.

ance of effort nowadays centers on work of a totally ornamental type.

The carving of wood for nondecorative purposes has practically passed from view. The shaping of religious figures by woodcarvers, once common in European history, has almost vanished entirely, and the carving of utilitarian objects has similarly diminished as wood has given way to other materials. Farm implements, printer's type, and numerous household utensils are seldom made the way they were originally. Of the few functional items still fashioned from wood, mechanical mass production has generally replaced the methods of handcrafting.

At organized woodcarver's shows, the wares are almost exclusively ornamental. Incised work and pieces embellished in relief are on hand, but attractively whittled and sculptured decorative pieces predominate. This is true throughout much of North America. Products having a utilitarian purpose are scarcely evident anywhere. Only in a limited number of places can craftsmen be seen customarily applying their skills to such things as the hewing of bowls and troughs from logs. Something similar may be said about the carving of logos and other symbols.

Designing for utility, unlike designing for decorative purposes, is both practical and aesthetic. An integral relationship exists between the form of an object and its use. The finished object must work as planned, and it must have a pleasing appearance. Thus, the artistic and technical aspects of design should be developed simultaneously. The function of the piece and its mass, shape, and balance must be kept in harmony as the work proceeds.

It should be no surprise that humorous whittlings and the more polished free-standing sculptures ordinarily fulfill a purpose of ornamentation. The experienced woodcarver will readily observe that many such carvings have no intended use besides their visual appeal. Judgment of the artistic worth of carvings in the round, therefore, frequently rests on principles applicable to decorative design. How appealing the finished figures will be may bear directly on the quality of the sketches made when designing.

Sketching Figures

Sketching has a basic purpose. Through sketching, the various features of a carving take shape. The lines define both form and detail.

In ordinary practice, the features of a proposed carving are first worked out on paper. Sketches are much more easily corrected than changes made while in the act of carving, which could be much more costly in terms of time and material; the pencilling of alternates on paper has practically no equal when making comparisons of different configurations. The ability to create an image directly on the wood develops as one gains confidence in his skill as a designer.

The beginner would be well advised to follow time-proven procedures. Observe the methods used to draw circles and ovals, as these constructions are fundamental to developing skill in figure sketching. Facility in sketching begins with learning pencil control. Illus. 3 and Illus. 4 illustrate how the constructions are drawn freehand, although there is certainly no rule against using a measuring device or a straightedge. Beginners usually find, however, that they are able to master the more speedy freehand method of construction.

Close observation of the drawings reveals that light-handed strokes have been used for blocking in, with firmer end-to-end strokes tracing the finished outlines. With experience, some circles and ovals will be sketched in place without the preliminary step. Whatever works will do. Craftsmen continually strive to simplify the effort required, because they can always return to the basic constructions when needed. The configurations are easily drawn to size and shape when constructed as shown in Illus. 5, and they should be practised often enough to develop expertise in their use.

The development of a technique for drawing circles and ovals is essential to figure sketching. Much of the difficulty of correctly posturing an animal of prey, say, in a stalking position is overcome by first drawing circles or ovals at the pivot points of the body, then outlining the head

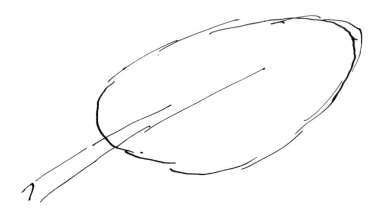

Illus. 3. Light pencilling usually precedes the more precise detailing of outlines.

Using radial lines to control size and shape

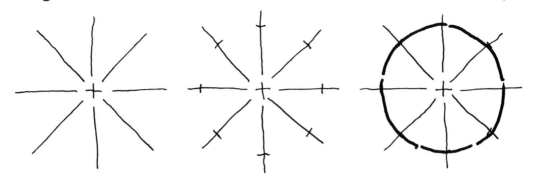

Sketching within a square

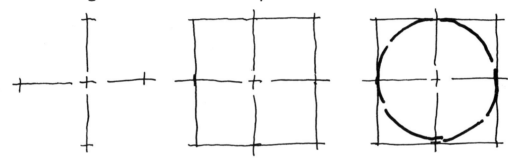

Sketching ovals by using parallelograms

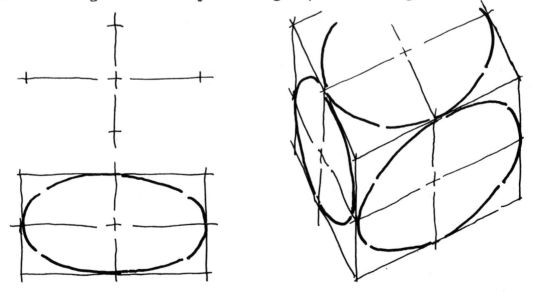

Illus. 4. Alternate methods of sketching circles and ovals preparatory to figure sketching.

SMALL DETAILS CAN MAKE A BIG DIFFERENCE

(a) Outline   **(b) Detail**   **(c) Show _mood**

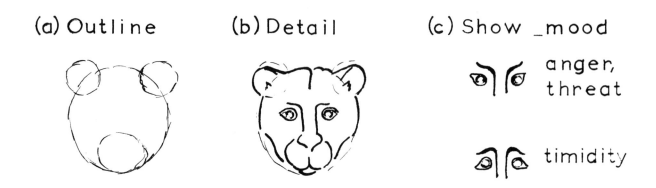

anger, threat

timidity

POSTURE <u>and</u> EXPRESSION CREATE CHARACTER

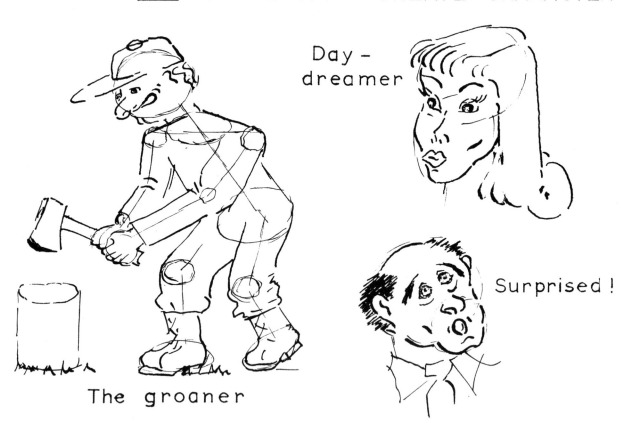

Day-dreamer

Surprised!

The groaner

Illus. 5. Some useful techniques in figure sketching.

and feet similarly. Finally, the lines needed for defining contour and detail are drawn.

After outlining, the final detailing takes place. Facial expressions become particularly important, for it is through the expression of an eye, the curling of an eyebrow, the furrowing of the forehead, or the twisting of the lips that much of the intended character will be displayed. A skilful whittler knows how easily slight changes in facial detail or posture can affect expressions of mood. Capturing the desired features in a sketch is a huge advantage (Illus. 5.). The point is not how prettily drawn is the object but how effectively represented are the features which impart character. A figure drawn without character will very likely be carved that way.

Several aids are helpful in drawing. When making freehand sketches, graph paper assists in keeping the views proportioned and aligned (Illus. 6.) Geometric figures, being composed primarily of arcs and straight lines, are most easily constructed with the aid of a ruler and mechanical drawing instruments. The requirements of precision and ease of construction must be considered when preparing a design.

Preparing Design Transfers

Once the design has been worked out by sketching, the final drawing must be produced on the wood. Outlines guide the carving. Several methods of transferring figures are in use, with the tracing of outlines being the most common.

Probably the easiest way to begin is to prepare a full-size layout on paper, and then position the drawing on the wood with a sheet of carbon paper in between (in place of carbon paper, the back side of the drawing's outline can be blackened with a lead pencil). Having so done, lay the design face upwards for tracing the figure in the proper position onto the wood (do this for both front and side views on a block of wood to be carved in the round). Details need be added only sparingly to a drawing for tracing, because most lines transferred to the wood are soon removed when carving.

Designs having duplicate parts need only be partially drawn, as shown in Illus. 7–9. The

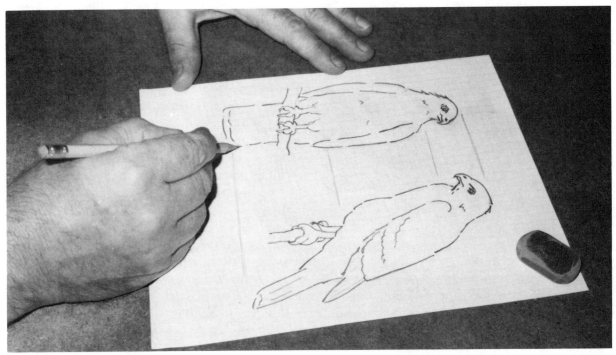

Illus. 6. The use of graph paper helps in maintaining proportion and alignment when sketching.

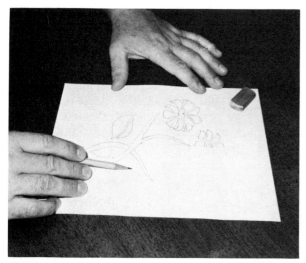

Illus. 7. Designs having matching parts need not be drawn completely when preparing a layout for transfer.

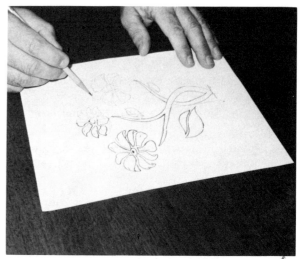

Illus. 9. The lines may then be darkened, or the figure may be traced onto the wood as it is.

Illus. 8. The paper can be folded and rubbed with the pencilled sections positioned where desired.

complete drawing results from transferring matching parts with the paper folded. By following this procedure, the designer has a better chance of maintaining the exactness desired. The process becomes most advantageous when duplicating entire halves of elaborate designs.

Practising Good Procedure

Mastery of the design process seems to be primarily the consequence of persistence and practice. Natural talent helps, but it does not take the place of diligent effort when learning. Learning to sketch reasonably well is only a start.

In actual practice, experienced designers occasionally lay their drawings aside and return to them later. Doing that enables them to view the work afresh. The technique has merit for everybody, but especially for learners.

The complete process of design has its beginning in the creative, intuitive, and analytical faculties of the mind. As the process develops, it further involves the mind in a series of decisions until a final conclusion comes forth. The similarity of the procedure to the scientific method of development may become evident in the sequence of steps below.

1. Define the purpose. Is it ornamental or utilitarian? What need will the carving fulfil?

2. Identify limiting facts. Where will the object be used? By whom? Any preferences of style? Any size, material, or subject restrictions to consider?

3. *Draw the details.* Make thumbnail sketches, beginning with known requirements. Create an appropriate form. Observe principles of balance, unity, proportion, etc.

4. *Select the best plan.* Is the most attractive drawing also the best plan? Is it within the capacity of the carver, the material, and the tools? Does it fit the purpose?

5. *Further analyze the plan.* Does the intended owner find the design appropriate? Are persons skilled in design available for comment?

6. *Finalize the design.* Modify the design if need be, reject it completely if necessary, or accept it and proceed.

There are many critical ideas suggested in the list, such as style and fundamental principles of design, that are discussed and illustrated in the following chapters.

II
STYLES OF CARVING

Styles vary according to taste and mores. Ethnic preferences differ and items fashionable in one country may be totally out of place in another. From time to time the choices of separate groups may undergo radical change, but the preferences of whole civilizations tend to modify at an incredibly slow pace.

Woodcarving practices vary similarly. Neither the reliefs and incised arabesques of Middle-Eastern cultures nor the symbolic twentieth-century carvings of New Zealand's Maoris are found much in Western countries, though foreign-made carvings do reach Western retail markets occasionally. Many from India are widely distributed in America, but they sell more for their low price than their artistic value. They are often made too elaborate, and the workmanship suffers from attention to quantity rather than quality of decoration. While some Indian work meets high standards, more of it would be acceptable in style and aesthetic treatment if the workmen were better schooled about Western taste. It is noteworthy how the practice has gone on for generations with no discernible change.

The trivet in Illus. 10 illustrates this point. Even though its features are relatively simple, the practice of embellishing pieces all over remains evident. Although a recent import, it is no different in quality or style from objects sold during the 1930s.

Illus. 10. An example of the lavishly detailed woodcarvings commonly imported for sale in this country.

American woodcarving follows no definite pattern. Highly diverse designs are produced in this country, but not one style has come into extensive use. Designs as divergent as the purely naturalistic and the purely abstract capture the craftsmen's fancy.

Classifying Designs

There are five types of design that have an objective basis: realistic, stylized, conventional, geometric, and abstract. Each of the five types requires some degree of arranging by the craftsman and so meets the main criterion of design, though not everyone will consider the results equal in visual appeal. Individual differences about quality in design are to be expected.

The five terms are useful identifiers of the principal features of the different carving styles, regardless of the variation of details within each category. Much confusion has developed because of a lack of clarification on this point. One authority may state that a particular carving is somewhat stylized or that it is severely stylized, while another will hold it to be made slightly, moderately, or severely abstract. Not only are the terms *abstract* and *stylized* often used interchangeably but also the two seem to be used at different times to describe virtually every design which has not been made naturalistic in style. Those positions may be actually correct for some fine arts applications. Still, the five classifications from the field of two-dimensional art gives the woodcarver a more descriptive and useful direction.

Illus. 11. Figures arranged, carved, and tinted in realistic style.

Designing Realistically

Realistic design is one step away from naturalistic reproduction. The difference is that it requires an artistic emphasis and interpretation by the designer. A realistic creation does justice to form as it exists, but the resulting carving does not have the same exactness of detail. Oftentimes the grain of the wood on a finished piece makes the difference.

The amount of deviation from the actual thing may be quite little, and it usually results from the woodcarver's technique. Illus. 11 shows this. The carvings are fixed in a manner portraying reality, with both the relative positions of the animals and their body attitudes adding to the realism of the composition. Illus. 12 shows several points of departure from naturalistic designing. The artificial appearance from the tool marks is a pronounced difference. There can be no doubt that these are carved animals. Acrylic tinting also reveals this. One need not hold or touch the figures to know they are made of wood. Visual inspection alone suffices.

In naturalistic carving, each minute feature is meticulously detailed in place, unlike the realistic carvings shown. Rather than reproducing nature exactly, only enough surface coloring is used to enhance the otherwise bland basswood. A minor contrast occurs as a result of the unnatural trimming of the branches. The smaller-than-life size of the animals, on the other hand, has no bearing on style at all. The subjects need only be kept in proportionate scale in both types of carving.

Illus. 12. Even bold cuts can portray the muscle tension and emotion of an actual confrontation.

Stylizing Animals

Illus. 13. Stylized carvings, such as this road-runner, are one step from realism.

Illus. 13 depicts a stylized carving of a roadrunner. A measure of continuity is achieved by basing the design on a generally recognized animal shape. The difference between the natural form and a stylization becomes evident in a comparison of a roadrunner in its natural habitat with this piece.

The carved roadrunner has distinctly realistic qualities in its general shape and posture, the setting in which it stands, and the color behind the eyes. These are much as they might occur in the wild. Yet, the carving goes beyond realistic styling. The buttonwood grain loosely indicates feathers and, more importantly, the intentionally contrived details of the tail, crest, and wings are special stylizations for purposes of effect and simplicity.

In stylized work, there is a visible presence of artistic license. Stylizing results from the designer exercising substantially more freedom of expression than attainable in a realistic portrayal. It embodies the idea of a design becoming a more important element when first, artistic interpretation exists—the designer shapes, distorts, or in some way emphasizes one or more features—and, second, truth of process and material occurs so that the final product does not appear to be an imitation. Purists contend a woodcarving should never be made to look like an object composed of another material or by another process. Their contention applies, with some notable exceptions, to practically any kind of carving.

Some artistry of application can be seen in most features in Illus. 13. The arrangement of grass for concealing prey, the deliberate stepping in a stalking posture, and the visual sleekness of a swift fowl are the major exemplifications. The clear, satin finish helps bring out the desired features.

The naturalistic spots of red and blue behind the subject's eyes have a special purpose. A touch of bright color added to a stationary subject tends to bring it to life and impart a dynamic quality.

Conventionalizing Carvings

Conventionalizing is designing in an unnatural, often formalized way. Formalization is not completely synonymous with conventionalization, but it describes much of the work done in the conventional manner. Repetition is an important part of it. Identical parts may be balanced about a centerline, or whole subjects may be repeated in more or less extensive patterns, as in Illus. 14A.

The process does not have exactly the same result as symmetry in animal forms. Most animals are symmetrical. One half usually has an image reversed about a vertical plane extending fore to aft. Illus. 14B includes an example. The symmetry of natural figures may be reproduced in designs of any type, and it will not determine a design's classification according to style. Nevertheless, subjects from nature are given symmetrical configurations more often in the conven-conventional style than in others.

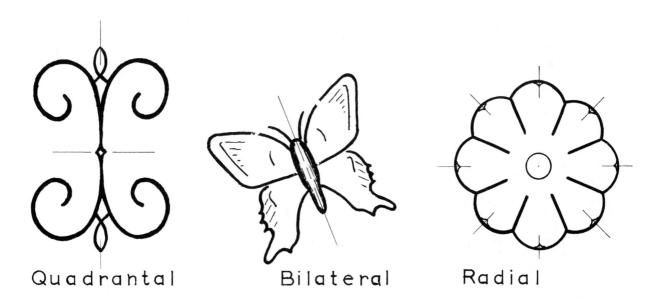

Quadrantal   Bilateral   Radial

Illus. 14. Symmetry of form in nature and design.

Normally, objects in nature show symmetry only in a general way. Differences are seen on close inspection. A good designer will take advantage of either quality, depending on circumstances, but he will frequently stress the bilateral convention of an animal or the radial repetitiveness of a flower by drawing some parts exactly like others. This forces the shape into a rigid pattern, as in Illus. 14C.

The arrangement in Illus. 15 has its basis in this style, the birds having been paired for effect in an orderly, formalized manner. Repetition occurs. The birds are similarly placed and have identical features and shapes, and their slightly distorted figures impart interest and attractiveness to the convention.

Is the subject matter appropriate for representation in this style? To answer that question, one should consider whether or not the carvings create the emotional feeling intended. The definite similarities within the composition seem to produce a sense of oneness. The treatment in Illus. 15 seems to accomplish this quite well. The wood, color, and natural finish combine in striking contrast. The redness of the cherry-wood pedestal comes vividly through the transparent finish. It effectively complements the whiteness of the birds. The buckeye, the wood from which the birds are carved, presents a picture of purity due to thorough bleaching and tinting.

Freedom to apply artistic talent abounds within very general limits when designing conventionally. Important rules must be observed. Repetition, balance, and formalization are points to consider. Conventional applications also require restraint or monotonously repetitive compositions can easily result.

Developing Geometric Figures

The application of geometry as a mode of expression presents another challenge to the designer. Mathematical models are applied in the graphic representation of theoretical constructions and

Illus. 15. A conventionalized assembly positioned to show two contours of the pear-shaped birds.

subjects from nature. Designs are built to form planar figures (lines, rectangles, circles, or ellipses) or solid constructions (cones, pyramids, and spheres).

Application of shapes to tangible objects in an artistically acceptable way can very definitely become a trial-and-error exercise. Unlike theoretical construction with its seemingly endless possibilities, designing from nature requires the fitting of an object into a geometric form while maintaining some likeness of the original. Because of this limitation, objective geometric design necessitates considerable ingenuity on the part of the designer.

Illus. 16. Simple elegance sometimes results from well-chosen combinations of geometric shapes.

A geometrically designed animal is presented in Illus. 16. Parts of circles and flat planes define the shape. No unique meaning is intended. The arrangement simply defines the creature in a familiar, static posture.

Several features of the design bear emphasizing. The intersecting perpendicular planes, the horizontal one on which the figure stands and the other extending vertically from it, reduce the potential for monotony that could have developed if it had been drawn with more arcs. The straight edges provide variety among the arcs. The perpendicular elements also infuse a degree of stability in the carving.

Perpendicularity, incidentally, is another useful technique in the artistry of design. One merely has to look about to see how common perpendicular planes and edges are in our environment and, thereby, acquire a feeling of how *right* they are.

Another point of interest is the placement of the animal's eye. What appears as a blackened pupil is actually a small knot in the pine. It is no accident that the mark stands out as shown. What might have been a sorely detractive blemish is now an integral part of the design. A careful woodcarver always remains alert to the opportunities the grain of the wood provides.

Abstracting a Subject

Although geometric designs of animals deviate markedly from natural form, designs completed in the abstract can represent an even greater departure. A subtle feature or two often remain as the only clue to the subject's identity. In some instances, the subject comes into view only by stretching the imagination.

An abstractionist has almost total freedom at his command. He creates virtually as he sees fit, insofar as he satisfies aesthetic requirements. The process becomes a way for him to make a visual statement. The statement may emphasize some physical detail, a special posture, or an interesting attitude relevant to the actual figure. Personal desires control the outcome, as long as cleverness doesn't replace effectiveness in an interpretation.

Objective abstraction always begins with an idea. Something comes to mind—a scene, a figure, an incident. A sort of mental manipulation takes place. The artist's individuality comes into play through his personality, emotion, and experience. A design eventually emerges as the illustrator strives to minimize external constraints. An assessment of the result rests almost entirely on use of the ideal elements of art.

The abstract style is comparatively difficult to master, for several reasons. No exact models exist, and the individualistic nature of an abstraction leaves little assurance the finished carving will be generally accepted. On the other hand, exact duplications of natural forms seem proper to practically everyone regardless of whether the subjects are attractive or unattractive.

Beginning designers should keep early abstractions simple. (As a rule, the simpler the design the better.) A figure uncomplicated in form is not necessarily easy or less worthwhile artistically. In fact, the exact opposite may be true. Sculptures are sometimes recognized for their outstanding gracefulness and simplicity of lines.

Illus. 17. An abstract figure has definite meaning when designed to suggest a subject.

An abstract piece done with minimal detail for the subject is shown in Illus. 17. The subtle shape and configuration about the eyes leave little doubt as to the subject's identity. The absence of sharply carved feathers, wings, and feet does not alter the expression, and any additional detail would probably detract from the central idea. This owl, apparently looking for the movement of prey, sits silently and endlessly leering downward. The stoic posture defines a customary part of an owl's life, and that is the idea. The naturally balanced mass, smooth contour, flowing surface, and complementarily curved eye-sockets produce the effect desired, with the other elements being simply suggested or left to the experience of the observer.

Selecting an Appropriate Style

Having five styles of objective design to choose from can be difficult. After all, the investment in the carving can be much too great to make a decision casually. The benefit of a client's specific order may alleviate the difficulty. Otherwise, the craftsman may have to rely on any personal preferences revealed, such as in the furnishings of the prospective owner's home.

Compatibility is important. A good designer considers where the piece will be displayed and if the area is traditional or modern, simple or elaborate, mixed or matched, or light or dark. Such information becomes most essential when dealing with an elegant decor. Without the desired harmony of taste, the carving will probably stand out as a conspicuous afterthought or, worse, an ugly addition. A reasonably sophisticated person need only imagine the carved artifacts in Illus. 18 in a place of modern design as evidence of such disharmony.

Illus. 18. Ornaments styled in the tradition of an earlier time should be applied to articles of appropriate style.

Sometimes a particular location becomes appropriate. The carved owl in Illus. 17 would look better on an elevated surface than on a low table. Whenever possible, the designer should consider the features of an object in relation to its placement.

Certain carvings look better when placed adjacent to another decoration, as in Illus. 19. This makes the wooden creation more of a part of the decor than an inordinately imposing piece standing alone.

Illus. 19. A carving placed in complementary surroundings makes the piece and the rest of the display more interesting.

Although sculptors frequently prefer to work without having to contend with restrictions, the woodcarver should first develop a solid reputation for quality before taking that as a firm position for commission work. Carving in complete isolation may satisfy one's ego, but it may also lead to the sheer neglect of more than just extraneous factors. Generally speaking, a carving should be made suitable for the surroundings— not the surroundings for the carving.

The designer must know the subject when styling objectively. The importance of such knowledge can be understated. Someone attempting to carve a stylized buffalo, for example, will likely achieve best results if he studies the features and habits of the animal in real life. Viewing the subject in its natural habitat is the best choice, but in many cases illustrated books and magazines are the only viable alternative.

How much preparation should precede the actual shaping of the wood depends on several slightly obvious factors. Assuming the job is considered to be an important one, the craftsman's skill and approach to the task are among the remaining variables of considerable consequence. Highly skilled persons will either make a scaled drawing, sketch a few lines directly on the wood, or develop clay replicas. The amount of experience a person has with a given method makes the difference. Lacking familiarity with a particular style of design, the craftsman should make several sketches at the very least. Not many can achieve good results with less effort.

Creating Different Types

Style applies without restriction. Relief and incised carvings, as well as those done in the round, lend themselves to categorization. Furthermore, the different applications need not be confined to animals or their facsimilies. For the sake of simplicity, the following presentations are limited to the conventional style.

In Illus. 20, as was true in the display of the paired birds, repetition and formal balance are dominant. While the motif is traditional, it does not replicate reality. The controlled configuration of the ribbon element makes it appear unnatural. Symmetry exists, but not about one axis alone. That condition makes the design suitable for use on projects customarily viewed from different angles.

Conventionalizing in this way produces a pattern of appropriate form for carving in relief. Notice that only about one-fourth of the pattern need be drawn on paper in a quadrantal layout.

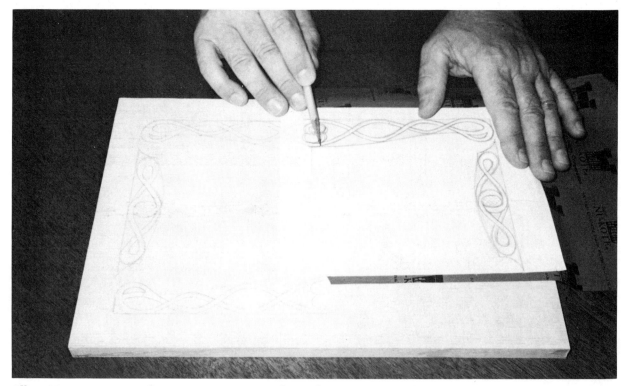

Illus. 20. Repetition and symmetry are commonly used conventions in designs for relief carving and incising.

Notice also that an objective styling need not have a natural origin.

Another variety of conventional styling is seen in the incising of the cherry-wood desk in Illus. 21 and Illus. 22. Here are previously explained aspects of the style, as well as a nonformalized balance not previously seen. Proper use of the technique does much to offset monotony. A matter of extreme importance is to place the balance point of such an arrangement, the center of mass, in a visually effective spot, which is well done in this application. The arrangement can be viewed comfortably from any position to its front.

Although not formalized symmetry, repetition is a fundamental feature in this composition. The leaves, stems, and flower heads display closely similar, and in some respects almost exact, shapes. The spacing of the flowers, their size, the numbers of leaves, and the shapes of petals introduce the element of variety. (From a construction standpoint, cherry wood serves beautifully both for fashioning as a practical piece of furniture and for decorating by carving. Its rich color and firmness are superb qualities.)

Illus. 21. An incised decoration, as applied to the desk leaf, need not be made elaborate to be effective.

Illus. 22. The nonformalized arrangement provides variety in a design of conventional styling.

III
PRINCIPLES
AND PROCEDURES

The principles of design are probably easier to understand and apply than most people realize. Although not everyone will become an expert, learning design depends more on desire and practice than on innate ability. Talented wood-carvers, in particular, should experience little difficulty in mastering the fundamentals.

The Basics

Designing, like all art, cannot be done strictly according to principles, or rules. Likewise, knowledge of the basics will not lead freely to outstanding results. Yet, to be applied properly, the basics must be understood. Once skilled in their use, the craftsman can then concentrate on the artistry of interpretation, arrangement, and expression. Having a finished carving actually convey some thought shows that the design work has gone beyond a mechanical application of formulas and rules.

The beginner will also learn the difference between man-made rules and natural laws: rules have exceptions; the laws of nature do not; and a rule may change completely while a natural law rarely changes. Such things as flower petals growing radially from a center and the earth's gravitational pull are constant and consistent. The various effects seem proper because, like the visible trail of a falling meteorite, they are physically factual.

Rules, however, do not have to be observed with unrelenting consistency. Exceptions are significant. A once common admonition of authorities never to place the main subject of a picture on center nor to illustrate predominately in monochromatic blue are rules which may be, and have been, broken by skilled hands. This is an important point, but rules generally have a worthwhile purpose. Persons at the learning stage, especially, should pay heed to them. Experimentation with the principles of art becomes more acceptable after establishing a reputation for achieving quality.

Quality ordinarily depends on observing a subject closely, reacting sensitively to it, and creating a visually communicative piece within the confines of accepted procedure. Design principles and constructs of imagination should be balanced in the process. Exclusive attention to seasoned authority and reasoned principles could result in a loss of individuality in the finished work, but too much reliance on the mind's intuitive and creative powers could result in oddly conceived, uncommunicative, overly personal forms of carving.

A good design comes about as much from feeling and responding as it does from applying principles. Skillfully carried out, a design can stimulate deep emotions in the viewer. Only rarely will a designer achieve the desired effect on the first attempt. Repeated practice and conscientious effort are customary bases of progress.

Establishing a Purpose

Early in the design process, a fundamental decision must be made as to the purpose. A project's intended use will bring one of several different parameters into focus.

The purposes of woodcarving fall into four general categories: for making pieces which are decorative by themselves; for shaping articles which serve a practical, or utilitarian, purpose; for applying decorations to articles of practical use; and for producing figures which have some spiritual or symbolic meaning.

The procedure for making a decorative article in relief is briefly presented in Illus. 23–26. Actually, the carving of a purely decorative article can be done by any of several methods.

Decorations for wall mounting are readily carved in relief, by incising, or by shaping in the round. Free-standing decorations in wood are usually whittled or sculptured.

Whether or not a piece carries a message or evokes a particular emotion does not alter the underlying purpose. Woodcarvings may elicit responses of humor, sorrow, revulsion, acceptance, laughter, etcetera, and still be decorative forms of art. The finished carving in Illus. 27 exemplifies something of special interest to most children. The exhibition of such objects, that is, pieces functioning primarily as works of art, has become so prevalent that no longer does their importance undergo questioning.

Without question, the carving of decorative pieces is one of the most important applications of woodcarving. The person who concentrates on this area of design must learn not only how to direct meaning and emotion into his work but also how to plan with assurance the materials and methods of construction specified that can do the same. In brief, he will not reach his full potential without knowing both purpose and procedure.

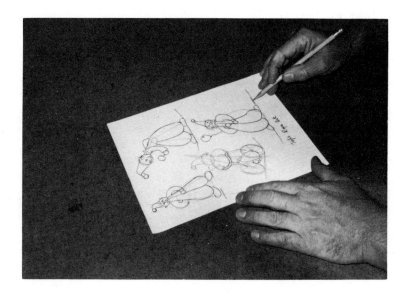

Illus. 23. As a matter of basic procedure, a design should be worked out so as to convey an idea in the manner intended.

Illus. 24. Lightly drawn outlines guide the shaping of figures while allowing for minor changes.

Illus. 25. The woodcarver must think in a three-dimensional mode as the background is leveled for texturing and the drawn lines are carved away.

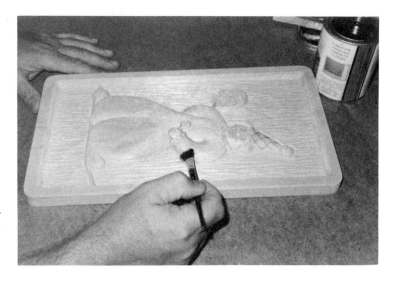

Illus. 26. Choices regarding the finish—here applying a sealer before painting—also have an important place in the design process.

Illus. 27. The finished "Act on the Low Wire" represents that class of woodcarvings made strictly for a decorative purpose.

Another distinct purpose of woodcarving is utility. Although useful products made of wood are becoming scarce, the designer must remain aware of the possibilities. The demand for hand-carved utilitarian pieces still exists for a few kinds of household items.

A product carved for some practical use should, first and foremost, satisfy the work requirement. The artistic aspects of design emerge with the technical in creating an article which both functions well and looks good. The fulfilment of practical use in an aesthetic form, rather than sheer decorative embellishment, must consume the attention of the designer. The utilitarian product derives its artistic value essentially from the form devised for the task.

Illus. 28 shows several useful applications of woodcarving. The handle of the letter opener provides for ease in gripping when opening mail, and the wooden base of the pen holder supplies the necessary support. Both are easily moved about. The firmness of material, smoothness of form, and configurations of shape are compatible, one piece with the other. Simple, round-edged blocks might serve about as well, but the rhythmic appearance in this set is much more artistic in styling.

Applying a decoration to an article of practical use is *not* the same as creating for utility. A properly made utilitarian article will function adequately with or without a decorative carving. No decoration of any kind should ever impede utility.

In general, a woodcarving should be applied to a useful piece only as an enhancement of an area that otherwise would be too plain. The wall-

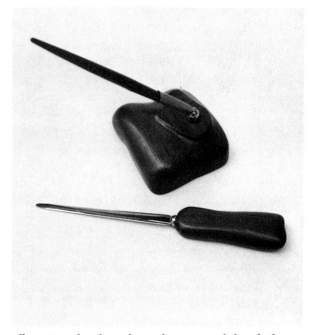

Illus. 28. The shaped wooden parts of this desk set are applications of the utilitarian purpose of woodcarving.

cabinet design in Illus. 29 makes this clear. Undecorated, the cabinet would be quite dull.

Doves, eagles, and lions are among the subjects sometimes given a spiritual or other intangible meaning. The figures are occasionally given three-dimensional form in wood for a purpose aside from mere enjoyment or use in a tangible kind of work. Their intended function of conveying a particular message and meaning places them in a special category. The religious implication of the cross is a powerful example. Company trademarks and symbols of fraternal organizations are other examples.

Arranging Basic Elements

The elements of design are best explained using simple configurations. Line, shape, and space arrangements are a beginning, though not all of the arrangements explained here apply with equal expressiveness in each type of carving. This usually becomes evident within the context given, as when referring to background which has relevance almost exclusively in relief carving.

The line is fundamental. It segments space, defines shape, shows movement in a given direction, and imparts a psychological meaning. While a vertical line seems to imply strength, a horizontal stroke appears restful, and the diagonal seems restless. Lines crossing produce tension. Illus. 30 shows some other meanings and uses. Their significance derives from the natural condition and order of things. The several arrangements clearly indicate the powerful effects possible in design, and how easy it is to create combinations which harbor an unintended or undesirable meaning.

When illustrating objects, how the shapes are drawn and how they appear in nature are often quite different. A technique used in two-dimensional art is outlining. It is used mostly for product drawing and sketching, specifically for representing edges, creases and general changes in contour. The line as such does not occur in nature. In relation to this, when one hears about a product having "good lines," it is the surface

Illus. 29. A third major purpose for carving wood is the decoration of articles made for practical use.

form and contour, rather than the lines *per se*, which actually evoke such comments.

Although outlining continues to be common in design, carving-tool cuts rarely replace only the lines as pencilled. The carving of outlines is mostly limited to the gouging of borderlines or to narrow incising about the edges of shapes. In relief carving, the drawn outlines give way when forming the surface limits. A study of a figure's outline as drawn on the wood in relation to work in progress indicates how the lines temporarily guide the carving.

Shape, or form, represents one of the most important considerations in carving, but something more must be present in a composition. For sculptured applications, attention must be centered additionally on the related matters of mass and contingent space. The position and surrounding area of a composition have a definite

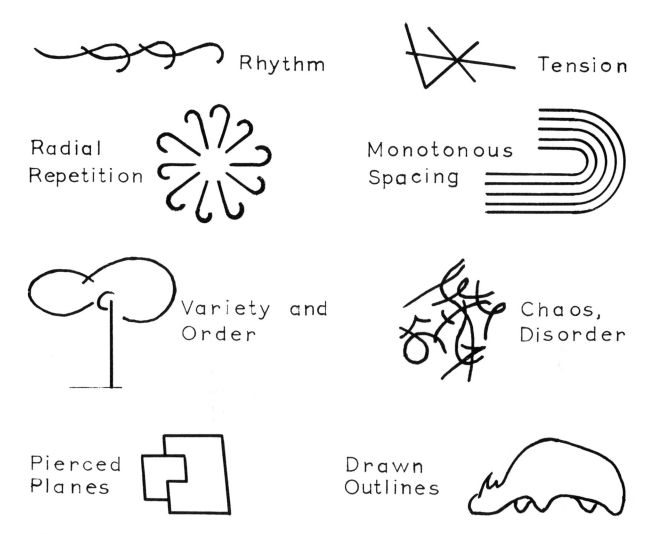

Rhythm

Tension

Radial Repetition

Monotonous Spacing

Variety and Order

Chaos, Disorder

Pierced Planes

Drawn Outlines

Illus. 30. Some aesthetic and psychological applications of lines.

relationship to shape in incised and relief carving.

Once again, look at Illus. 24 for a study of form, position, and background in a conventionalized relief carving.

The area around a carved object needs special attention. Surrounding space affects a composition nearly as much as form itself. An equally divided background area may be comprehended without much mental effort, while a diversity of areas can seem more stimulating and interesting.

Formalized carvings are limited in this respect. This shortcoming is somewhat offset by the apparent stability and precision of balance in that kind of design.

The direction of certain cuts can give the appearance of motion or stationary positioning. Straight cuts seem to be fixed when butting against a boundary, and V-cuts placed parallel to the sides likewise have a static quality. A sense of movement results from having curves and shadows angled within a form instead of merely

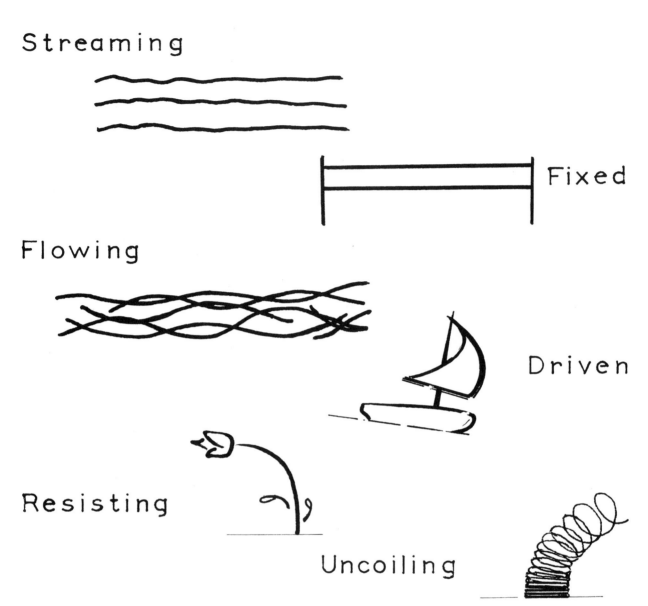

Streaming

Fixed

Flowing

Driven

Resisting

Uncoiling

Illus. 31. Techniques for portraying motion and stability.

outlining it. Curves portray movement more effectively than do straight cuts, although the two provide a pleasing contrast when used in combination. Some applications of these points are shown in Illus. 31. The objects show the results of applied force. The designer should learn to represent such conditions, whether by dynamic positioning or by subtle implication.

Unity in a composition represents another kind of force—one which relates to the principles of harmony and congruity and applies in relief carving as in two-dimensional art. A good design instills a feeling of coherence among its parts. An object located closer to the border than to other objects in a group fails to provide the sense of togetherness of a unified design. Ordinarily, the area surrounding a group should be greater than that between or among the objects within. Points of interest far apart or different-looking similarly lack a unified appearance, unless a counteractive force has been introduced by repeating some strong element of the shapes.

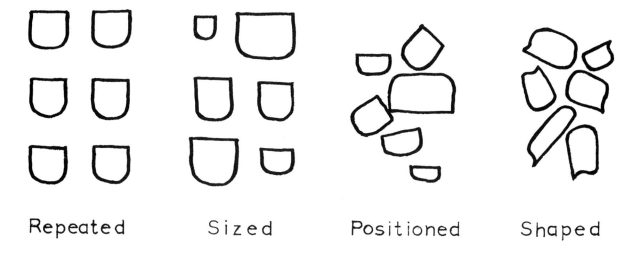

Repeated   Sized   Positioned   Shaped

Illus. 32. Variations created from a static grouping.

The repetition of too much detail in a carving results in a dull and uninteresting piece. Variety counteracts that effect. Altering the sizes and shapes of objects or areas, breaking-up the regularity of intervals, or making radical changes in the subject are all ways of achieving variety. However, eliminating sameness altogether may again lead to a loss of unity. Illus. 32 presents the main ideas.

The learner should remain cognizant of the fact that the sereneness of a static effect may be intentional and entirely acceptable, for not every design must be radiant with energy. The designer has to determine what is appropriate. Any mood at all may be expressed, as long as it fits the subject.

Positioning Subjects Effectively

Positioning is closely related to spacing. Selecting the proper location for a subject or main feature is a customary part of pictorial design. Careful observers know that pictures are often mounted with a larger border below than along the sides and top. This holds the composition optically on center and thereby creates a sense of stability instead of slipping. The wall-cabinet design follows this practice. Compositions without such spacing along the borders must be designed internally so that the mass seems stable.

The exact location of the optical center depends on the size and nature of the work. This location cannot be determined by measuring, since placing the center of mass a distance much above a line extending horizontally through true center could be as visually disturbing as providing insufficient distance. The rule of locating a center of force above true center, at the risk of sounding obvious, applies solely to decorations intended for vertical display. The acceptance today of a design's placement in a corner far removed from the midpoint does not negate the importance of optical centering generally.

When positioning the main subject in a nonformalized design, look for the "golden cut." This particular spot may be observed in many types of pictorial drawings from the recent past. The golden cut falls in an area measured from two-thirds to three-fourths along the side of a rectangular boundary. Less attention is paid to this principle now than before, but purposeful applications still appear. If that is used or not, a subject must be oriented for complementary support by the subordinate elements of the composition.

The positioning of planar figures parallel to the background of a carving has an effect different from those placed at an angle. The former appears static, and the latter seems to indicate movement. Oblique planes show direction as well.

Point of view, perhaps as much as anything else, must be kept in mind when designing for carving. Both individual figures and complete scenes require careful placement. Some figures may be viewed with pleasure from many angles, but others look best when placed in a certain position. For example, a bouquet in a stationary vase looks best if carved for vertical mounting, but would rarely be laid in the horizontal. It should never appear upside down to the viewer. If these conditions cannot be met reasonably well, as could be the case with the carving on a serving tray or box lid, choose a different design.

A carving's position affects appearance as much as the decoration itself. Poor placement detracts from both the design and the object it decorates. Stepping back and observing is a good way to check this. Anyone who has ever carefully hung a picture knows how well this works. Insofar as possible, decisions about position should be made during the drawing stage.

Fitting to Form

A decoration must fit the form of the object. Combining incongruous shapes is not unlike placing a square peg in a round hole. There must be compatibility. The carving and the outline of the surface it decorates should make an articulate combination. Illus. 33 gives an example.

The shape around the edges requires aesthetic treatment. At the design's boundary, the internal features should be muted so that the eye dwells on the subject. Having extensive numbers of shapes emanate from the edges will be generally undesirable, and having elements pointing so as to carry the line of sight directly out the corners will be disastrous. Any sense of unity, coherence, and emphasis can be completely lost. To have a single feature appear even remotely disturbing affects the entire composition. The artistry of the relief carving on the napkin holder conforms to these recommendations. While the balanced design radiates outward, it maintains a solidly unified appearance.

Up to this point, the subject of fitness has been applied only to decorative carvings. When a carving will be made for a functional purpose, it should then comply with the principles of utilitarian design. The primary objective in such design is to make the form fit the use.

Illus. 33. A carved design's placement, outline, and depth must fit the article.

Designing for Carving

Regardless of the style of a design, the method used to do the carving makes a difference. Differences occur in time and appearance. The careful use of speedy power tools produces unusually smooth surfaces, while textures ordinarily remain from handwork in relief and incising. Seldom are hand-tooled carvings finished to the smoothness of machined carvings. The variation, though often very slight, bears consideration when deciding on the design.

The craftsman will sometimes sand his carvings to the desired smoothness. Such work requires utmost care because excessive or careless sanding produces an unintended dullness of points and edges. Sculptured pieces are commonly sanded to remove tool marks. In other kinds of jobs, the probability of removing all tool marks remains quite small. When incising in a line with a router, for instance, a telltale roundness occurs at the ends of the cut. That detail could be eliminated with a chisel, but any unwanted deviation may remain permanently incised.

In relief carving, opportunities to correct miscuts are very prevalent. A high-speed cutting burr will level out a surface almost without leaving any evidence. Equally smooth cutting can be achieved by hand tooling in a meticulous paring action. For good reason, though, the extensive paring of wood has questionable merit. Time is one concern, but the main drawback is that the extra care does little more than remove a quality which gives a woodcarving its distinctly individualistic character. A rough texture also does much to hide miscuts while imparting a unique appearance.

Not everyone will agree on the relative merits of hand-versus-power carving. That seems inevitable. The issues can be debated extensively. In consideration of the possible arguments, one thing emerges above all else: If a woodcarving is to be made to look like a product of power tools, it might as well be made that way.

Most of the carvings shown in this book are the result of hand tooling, and the few exceptions are so noted. Evidence of handcrafting comes into view on close inspection of some of the photographs. In most instances, the emphasis centers on the aspects of design as opposed to carving procedures.

Maintaining Proportion

A keen, almost uncanny, sense of proportion must be developed for the objective representation of objects. Designers working in a realistic style have models in nature for comparison, while those forming caricatures and abstract figures frequently distort a feature or two. Some designers completely distort reality. Regardless of the approach, the need is to be aware of the actual sizes of objects and their parts in relative position—the balance of an arrangement depending on such knowledge. The relative amounts of mass and space in a piece far removed from the obvious must similarly be kept in proper relationship.

The impact of a disproportionately designed object may be realized by considering an oddly drawn oak-leaf cluster with acorns. Imagine the acorns to be as large as the leaves. Since acorns naturally grow among mature leaves, this simple example sends a very disturbing signal to the viewer. The eye keeps returning to the oversized shapes. In a good design, the eye will move about the whole composition without focusing for long on a single detail. Even a slight imbalance in the sizes of natural forms seldom escapes a critical viewer's attention.

At one time in the development of their art, the Greeks and Romans attempted to overcome the problems of balance by reducing the practice to mathematical proportions. A human figure, for instance, was scaled 7½ to 8 heads high. Interestingly, the present-day system of English measurement was derived to a notable extent from the dimensions of human anatomy.

Geometric shapes were also reduced to mathematical formulas. The purpose was to define shapes precisely in the name of beauty. One result was the golden rectangle. A rule of proportion, the golden rectangle has an arithmetic ratio of 1 to 1.618 along its sides. For practical purposes, this ratio may be approximated at 5 to 8. Another shape preferred in ancient times was the 9–to–20 rectangle. Some fixation on these proportions seems to have developed throughout the years.

Although the formulas are appropriate for occasional use today, the measurements need not be taken precisely in the ratios given. An ever-present danger is that the shapes will be used too freely and to the exclusion of all others. This would cause not only monotonous repetition of identical form but also a dysfunctional effect from forcing objects into certain proportional dimensions. Repeated application of a monotonous detail from object to object could be as disconcerting as its repetition within a figure.

Achieving Balance

The need to study one's surroundings and to look beyond those things which first become evident

should not be underestimated. The nature of balance has special importance here, for its understanding depends on both observation and imagination.

Objects in balance are in equilibrium. Two weights on a uniform beam provide a common illustration. When supporting equal weights, the fulcrum (supporting pivot) has to be midway between the two. If the weights are unequal, the fulcrum will have to be closer to the larger one in order to remain stable. The exact physical location of the pivot in a stable arrangement falls at a point at which the weights are equal in moment, that is, where the product of each weight and its distance to the pivot is the same on both sides. In the condition of dynamic balance, as with birds in flight, stability of motion derives from invisible forces.

An ability to sense the correctness of balance of any kind falls on the shoulders of the designer. Illus. 34 portrays a state of static balance. Were the condition physically unstable, the carving would seem about to drop from its support. Its stability seems obvious. The wind-blown flower in Illus. 31 (page 35) elicits a different feeling. Its

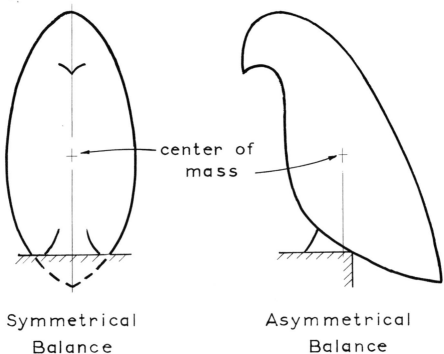

Symmetrical
Balance

Asymmetrical
Balance

Illus. 34. Physical and visual stability in a stationary figure.

rium results from the resistance of the underground root structure. The balanced forces in this illustration are sensed, rather than revealed. Unlike the statically positioned bird, with its center of mass directly over the base of support, the flower would appear to be blown completely out of balance were it not for the viewer's familiarity with the natural forms of dynamic balance.

In addition to knowing the physical variations, the designer must be able to assess the apparent forces of color, stress, area, and detail in a composition. Anticipating how the depth of shadow lines in a carving will affect compositional balance constitutes a peculiar requirement for the designer. Symmetrical designs do not pose the same problem as most other arrangements, because compositional balance and physical balance seem to coincide. The viewer is left with little doubt about that. An asymmetrical design, on the other hand, requires much more mental effort and intuitive feeling when evaluating the adequacy of its balance.

Showing Distance in Carving

Designs portray distance for purposes of realism. Applications commonly occur in artists' paintings. Most woodcarving offers fewer possibilities for showing distance than does painting, and the possibilities are more limited in carving in the round than in relief carving. Applications in incising are bound to an occasional pictorial representation.

Relief carving offers the woodcarver his greatest opportunity for showing distance, because designs in relief present almost as many opportunities for representing distance as painting does. Changes in size, position, detail, and direction, along with perspective, comprise the several ways to depict linear space or an expanse of area in these mediums. The practice of shading paintings makes a difference.

Methods of representing distance are shown in

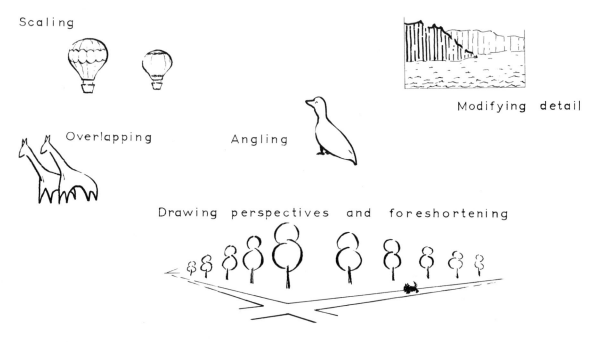

Illus. 35. Ways to depict distance in carving design.

Illus. 35. Creating actual distance by carving some parts more deeply than others becomes most effective when used in combination with the several methods. Many times, the desired effect can be obtained by altering the depth of cut a mere fraction. Depth of cut seems to compensate for shading with dark paint.

Designers should learn to use perspective with artistic skill. Few instruments are needed. Perspectives having either one or two vanishing points on the horizon may be readily sketched with the aid of a ruler, provided the designer understands the principles involved. Neither the ground plane nor the horizon line should coincide with a scene's border. Other than this, the rules of mechanical perspective generally apply.

Illus. 36. Compositional balance and style of design are not always fully apparent to the viewer.

In some carvings, depth and perspective are virtually impossible to represent. Certain incised designs make such detailing nearly or completely out of the question. The design on the corner shelf in Illus. 36 is one in which some depth has been represented in the roundness of the pine cone, but any remaining sense of depth or distance stems from the viewer's imagination. In stylized carvings of this kind the suggestion of the feature is enough.

Several factors worth considering went into the design and construction of the corner shelf. Pine was selected for its compatibility with the design, and the needles and cones were incised because of the relatively thin wood and for the appropriateness of the method in the area to be decorated. A coat of light-colored stain was applied after carving to make the design stand out more prominently. The application, when considered with the placement and style of the design, made an interesting and effective enhancement of the project.

Many of the methods of design originated long ago. The Renaissance gave rise to perspective, for example. The technique was applied continuously thereafter—a fact which stands as proof of the lastingness of certain principles. While the best principles of design have survived the spread of time, designs themselves seldom have had such consistent application. The usual practice has been to modify features from one period to the next.

Except in special circumstances, the accomplished craftsman will usually reject designs styled in the tradition of a long-gone period or distant culture. A vivid exception occurs when making authentic reproductions of works for inclusion with others of the same period.

The exciting thing about most designing is that an imaginative person need not duplicate previous work. The variations possible have practically no limit and each new project can be another creative experience. Form, subject, and style differences, when applied in conjunction with the several types of carving covered hereafter, represent a wealth of unique possibilities for the craftsman.

IV
RELIEF-
CARVING APPLICATIONS

Relief carving provides an exceptional opportunity for artistic expression. Not only does it make possible the creation of scenes similar to those painted on canvas, the woodcarver can actually produce depth of form rather than just an illustration. That capability is notable. While relief carving produces a uniqueness of form, shadow lines and background texture add an intrinsic quality not obtainable by any other method. The finished applications appeal to both the visual and tactile senses.

Relief carving, its advantages notwithstanding, imposes several limitations on the designer. For one thing, the shallowness of relief restricts the shaping of most objects of relatively large scale, including human figures. Better shaping, with depth kept in proportion, can be achieved by carving such figures in the round.

Color imposes another limitation. Whereas the painter enjoys considerable liberty in this area, the woodcarver uses color sparingly on subjects done in relief—if he uses it at all. As a rule, one working in relief must follow the principles of pictorial art rather consistently. The use of color may be the exception.

Knowing the Variations

In addition to an understanding of the principles of art, the designer must know the possible variations of relief work. Substantial differences occur throughout the range of high and low relief and as a result of the amount of roundness produced along the edges. Each variation should be considered for the unique opportunities it affords the designer for artistic expression.

High relief, or *bold relief*, defines one classification. The term represents a kind of carving in which half or more of a shape's depth extends above a background. The figures are sometimes undercut. When the background level falls at mid-depth of a shape, the name *half relief* applies. A form of high-relief carving may be seen in decorations involving piercing. In such work, portions of the wood are completely cut away.

Illus. 37 and Illus. 38 show a relief carving of an arrangement in buckeye, indicating how patterns take shape in a stylization of flowers. The strength of the shadows reveals the boldness of the carving. Placement of the flowers in parallel planes and squarely in front of the background follows a common practice. As in many other relief carvings, elements of pictorial art and sculpturing combine to form the composition.

Carving in shallow relief is often referred to as *low relief*, or *bas relief*, a practice especially useful for decorating thin-wood products. Figure projection remains slight when so carved, but not as shallow as in the *stiacciato* applied in the illustrations on coins. Low relief may be used by itself throughout a decoration, or it may be used in combination with the deeper cuts.

Illus. 37. Woodcarvers working in bold relief will occasionally sketch in part of a design as the work progresses.

Illus. 38. Freedom to create floral forms in a quasi-natural style immeasurably increases a designer's potential.

Illus. 39 (below). The carving of wood after first lightly applying a stain need only be very shallow for effect.

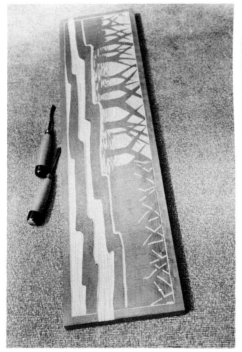

Illus. 40 (above). The finished composition, "Spring of '44," represents flooding by having carved the flat surface in a manner suggesting motion, space, and distance among the shapes.

Illus. 39 contains a design being carved by a special method. Artistic qualities aside, the carving is simplistically done in essentially two planes. The finished product is seen in Illus. 40. This method of carving seems to be the easiest in that the tooling leaves flat shapes at an elevation above a second plane. Such areas may be either deeply or shallowly carved. Stain, or paint thinly applied, often becomes an indispensable addition when creating by the two-plane method. The necessary contrast may be absent without it.

The flat shapes left by shallow two-plane carving are not at all foreign to the average viewer of works of art. The carving around the trees in Illus. 40 serves only to define contours by removing areas of surface stain. The result seems quite proper, in spite of any unnaturalness from the lack of roundness in those objects. The human eye has become accustomed to viewing shapes done in the flat, provided they contrast with their surroundings. Planar figures of different designs woven into tapestry, printed on wallpaper, and inlaid or painted on wooden boxes all show this. No shading need be added. The static positions of trees, the moderated flow of flood waters among them, and the surging action of swelling waters as gouged in the area of what would be a stream seem all to come into view without further realistic detail. The use of carving to represent a continuous flow from right to left is also evident.

Illus. 41. Plant life is a useful source of ideas for relief carving design.

Collecting Design Ideas

Besides knowing the potentialities of the several relief carving techniques, the designer needs an ability to develop creative ideas from his surroundings. Just about anything he sees is worthy of consideration. Objects as large as an imposing skyscraper and as small as a microscopic section of a flower stalk are within the range of possibilities for design. Both natural and man-made subjects lend themselves to modification for carving.

The natural world abounds with beauty. The frequency of biological forms in design motifs is evidence of that widely held view. Plant and floral life commonly serve as the basis for relief carving, while animal forms, due to their mass, seem to be best re-created in whittled and sculptured applications.

The serious designer would do well to make sketches of things of interest to him. These might show the shapes observed and any modifications intended for eventual recall. The natural forms in Illus. 41 suggest only a few of the many possibilities.

Capturing Natural Form

The matter of balanced growth in nature must be given careful attention by the designer. Some objects appearing to be symmetrical may not be so. This phenomenon allows for a certain amount of freedom in representation. Symmetrical balance may be portrayed or avoided. The human figure is a good example. It may be drawn in a frontal view with each half an image of the other or, as would be more likely in a close resemblance, be made with the two halves different in detail. In many instances, symmetry is less important than showing an emotional expression and appropriate posture.

As it is with detail within an object, so it is with detail among the same kind of objects. One flower in a scene could be made like another, but a realistic reproduction of those flowers would reveal a distinctive difference. Duplicity of form among objects gains attention in the more conventionally styled applications. Repetition in symmetrical form must be present in a formalized convention, but such balance has no essential place in most other applications.

The balanced order of symmetry is so pleasing to the eye that we commonly manufacture objects that way and arrange our possessions accordingly. One need only look casually about the home for examples. The range of symmetry implied here may be observed in chairs, among a group of them, and even in the way they are normally arranged about a table. Not many elements of design are more widely observed in everyday life.

Style in relief carving closely approximates that applied in other kinds of carving, although a strictly natural reproduction cannot be made in relief. The surrounding wood or textured background prohibits an exact portrayal of nature. Because of this, the realistic style comes as close as possible in relief carving to duplicating the actual thing.

When designing in the realistic style, an observant person will choose a subject which can be appropriately arranged and detailed. A climbing vine affords an excellent source of inspiration and opportunity for arrangement. A vine with a rhythmic flow from one border to another, as in Illus. 42, will tie separate parts together in a strong, unifying force. When made to climb upward, as if reaching for the sun, the vine and its attached leaves can be systematically reduced in size. This effect simulates growth and natural perspective at once. Boldly carved details add to the realism.

Illus. 42. A realistic carving in redwood showing elements of design interpretation and arrangement.

The grapevine in Illus. 42 derives much of its character from the depth of carving and background treatment. The vine and its leaves stand out boldly. Contrast between the coarsely textured areas and the smooth details produces a desired point of interest, and the deeply cut features provide the effect necessary for viewing the contours fully in a dark wood. Only the completeness of the bunches of grapes must be sensed.

The grape clusters, a principal feature of the carving, are placed in strategic positions to help keep the composition balanced and stabilized. The shapes contrast prominently with the surrounding elements such that the impact of the relationships constitutes the primary reason for the off-center positioning of the clusters.

The redwood has another effect. The aged board with its brighter inner structure imparts a subtle contrast to the carving. Of greater importance is the fact that thoroughly dried redwood easily crushes and splinters. The craftsman should consider those matters beforehand. He should not attempt to use such wood if the design requires very fine detailing.

The popularity of designing from nature comes from the frequently occurring contrast and variety of things. Contrast and variety can be produced in designs of all kinds by altering lines, forms, and textures. The object is to avoid unwanted monotony of detail. The desired effect can be obtained simply by using opposites side by side, such as large/small, rough/smooth, straight/wavy, cross-hatched/plain, flat/creased. When making a selection, the suitability of the combination for carving and for the composition becomes a highly important consideration.

Varying Natural Form

The form of an object depends largely on style. Style denotes the manner in which the designer chooses to do his work. While some develop their expertise along a single line, others strive to produce in different ways. Either is acceptable, but a change in style adds variety to the design process. The designer's personal slant will tend to give a finished piece an individualistic quality in any interpretation.

Persons seeking more liberty of arrangement than attainable through the realistic style may prefer an interpretation which maintains elements of realism but has a distinctively stylized appearance. The desk-top accessory in Illus. 43 has as its decoration a grouping of this kind. The composition is a moderate stylization which closely resembles a realistic carving of leaves and berries.

Illus. 43. This desk-top accessory has been decorated with the kind of stylized design that maintains features closely resembling reality.

An analysis of the carving reveals several features not found in nature or realistic design. The fruit clusters and leaves form a combination unlike any real thing, and the arrangement conforms to a rectangular outline. Such styling is entirely acceptable, while effectively removing the composition from the realistic category. Designs of this type fall at a level of abstraction between the realistic and conventional styles.

In conventionalized designs, the elements of true form become even less prevalent. Oftentimes the subjects are formalized and self-contained. If formalized, the parts rigidly balance about a dividing line. If self-contained, the subjects remain within themselves and do not appear to extend beyond any of the boundaries. The difference between a self-contained design and one that is not may be seen in a comparison of Illus. 42 and Illus. 43.

As previously mentioned, floral motifs appear quite commonly in relief carving. The shapes are easily created by this method, for the usual depth of cut is sufficient for detailing essential parts of a plant. Flowers and leaves have dimensions such that even shallow carving will adequately accommodate them in positions flat with the surface. An example is seen in Illus. 44.

on a flat surface upon which some object will be placed. The serving tray fulfills that criterion. The flatness of the design and its shallowly cut background provide a useful measure of stability and durability under repeated use. Never should a deeply carved, intricately shaped design extend into an area likely to be used for supporting some object. Not only would this overdecorate, but

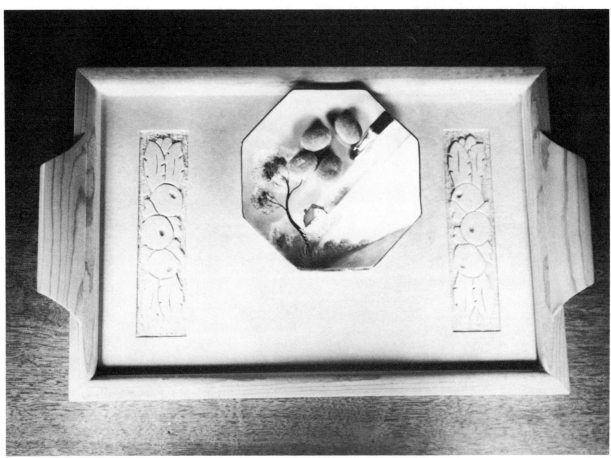

Illus. 44. The flat surface of a serving tray is an appropriate location for a shallow, two-plane conventionalized carving.

The kind of carving in Illus. 44 is a two-plane application in low relief. The background shows the effect of extremely shallow gouging followed by roughening with a knife point. Both this decoration and the one in Illus. 43 are appropriate on projects likely to be viewed from different directions.

The use of shallow relief, as in Illus. 44, has a distinct advantage in certain applications. This kind of low relief carving has a beneficial purpose

wearability would suffer.

The design on the serving tray represents another modification of nature due to conventionalization. The subject can hardly be mistaken for something other than botanical, even though nothing like it exists in nature. As customarily happens, the conventionalized motif has a place one more notch closer to the abstract than a stylized design.

Abstracting Natural Form

Geometric design moves boldly into the realm of the abstract. The shaping of flowers, foliage, and fruit to fit a geometric configuration produces a uniquely contrived appearance. The arabesques of the Middle East provide an effect far from that occurring naturally. Likewise, modern configurations utilizing the shapes of plane and solid geometry involve some distortion of ordinary growth. Certain shapes seem less strange than others when so used, such as the spherical and cylindrical forms which abound in nature. Flat planes of any great size, by way of contrast, do not occur naturally.

The process of geometric design involves a sort of forced shaping. Illus. 45 contains an example. Circles, cylinders, spheres, and straight cuts complete the essential parts of the floral design. The convexly and concavely shaped units display a bit of variety, with further contrast resulting from the stippling of the background.

Actual carving of the design follows the procedure of outlining the subject with sharp cuts,

Illus. 46. An abstract motif of simple design produces an effective decoration on this silverware chest.

tooling away the surrounding wood, and stippling the tooled areas with a large nail pointed to the desired shape. The floral units are then detailed. In the process, the boundaries of the carved areas and edges of the project are to be kept in harmony. The filler cuts (vertical grooves) along the sides are added in order to maintain a proper articulation of shapes. Doing that avoids a possible distortion of the design by widening.

Unlike designing geometrically, considerable license is permitted when designing completely in the abstract. The designer may apply his talent about as he wishes, while observing those principles which pertain to the decoration of wooden projects. He may, of course, shape a known subject into a configuration of his own discretion. How fitting the result depends on the skill of the designer in meeting the purpose intended.

The silverware chest in Illus. 46 bears analyzing for appropriateness of the design. First of all, the apparent simplicity of the decoration negates any feeling of overdesign. Secondly, the placement of the carving avoids the starkness of formalization. Thirdly, and aside from the apparent botanical motif, the abstraction has no sig-

Illus. 45. A stippled background makes an interesting contrast to the rigid appearance of this geometrically styled design.

nificance except to be reasonably compatible with the decoration on the utensils the box is to hold. The design's balance, shape, unity, and general arrangement is most pleasing to those favoring the less traditional type of styling.

Using Symbols in Carving

As an emblem, the symbol is a visible object with a second meaning. Tangible objects which stand for ideas, qualities, organizations, and the like, often become accepted through conventional usage, such as the eagle representing the United States and the dove signifying peace. To distinguish their organizations, many fraternal groups display emblematic signs (Illus. 47), and corporations often adopt symbolic trademarks by which they want to be known. Even the once common practice of craftsmen placing individualized identifying marks on their products has not completely passed from view.

The everyday world holds so many symbols that the person doing extensive design work can scarcely avoid them. Their high incidence and seemingly constant presence can profoundly influence one's efforts. Loose approximations of commonly known symbols, or even unlawful duplications, could creep unintentionally into the work of the unobservant person.

Well-known symbols require extra care (Illus. 48). The shapes must meet prescribed standards, and they should be displayed where appropriate. Registered trademarks may be used only under permissible conditions, but symbols in the public domain are open to unrestricted use and alteration when designing woodcarvings.

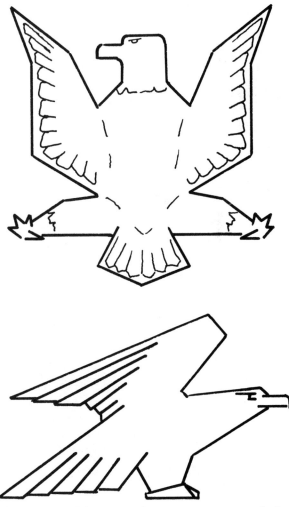

Illus. 48. Modifications of certain common symbols may occur without loss of identity or meaning.

Illus. 47. The symbol of a student's scholastic fraternity carved from mahogany in combined forms of relief.

For some applications, symbols do not have to be limited to conventional or traditional objects. The craftsman may create designs of his own. When doing so, his initial concern is to develop a form which has an apparent relationship to the thing being represented. The identifying signs of restaurants, resorts, and cottages offer opportunities for such expression. A unique name, location, or service may also suggest a symbol.

Piercing in Relief

The piercing of relief carvings produces a special effect. It incorporates procedures generally applicable to bold relief, but in this process wood is cut clear through at points not needed to hold the carving in place. The technique leaves each figure shaped partly in the three-dimensional manner of sculpturing. Illus. 49–52 give the basic steps.

Illus. 49. Pierced carving originates in a design of a special variety.

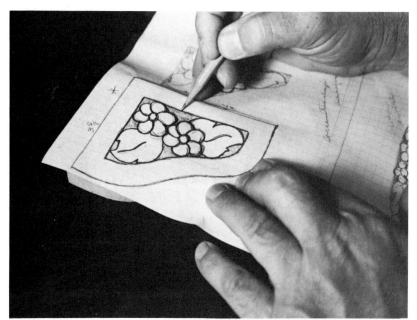

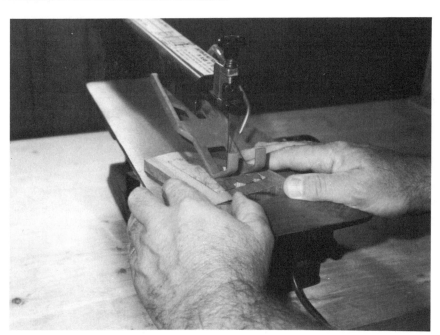

Illus. 50. Unwanted background can be readily removed with a scroll saw.

Carvings of this kind may be considered to be sculpturing, since pierced work in relief resembles carving in the round more than any of the others. Much of the surrounding wood will always be removed, and the shaping will usually proceed from more than one side. While, a carving in the round has no unaltered surface, a figure pierced in flat wood presents two principal sides at most. Usually, a pierced carving decorates an object instead of being an ornament which stands alone.

However applied to a project, a pierced design requires drilling and fine sawing to remove unwanted wood. A firm wood, such as cherry, will provide the strength and sharpness of detail needed. The choice of design again depends on the thickness of wood. The selection must ordinarily permit the carving of figures as fully as possible. In place of carving opposite sides of each figure as was done in the wall shelf (Illus. 53), double-faced designs may be carved at the

Illus. 52. The finished wall shelf reveals the carved work on both sides of each bracket.

51

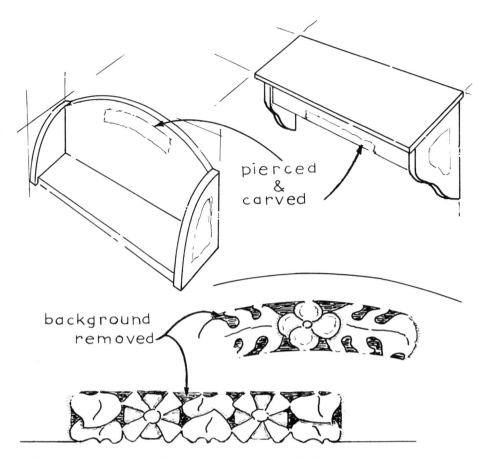

pierced
&
carved

background
removed

Illus. 53. Applications of designs in the pierced carving of wall shelves.

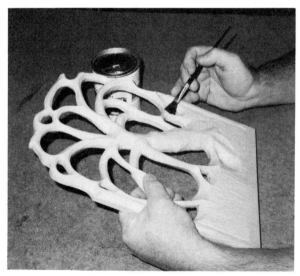

Illus. 54. Applying a clear finish to a pierced carving, "Waterside Willow," which emphasizes rhythmic form and space relationships in an informally balanced composition.

pierced locations. Of course, reverse sides need be carved only if both surfaces are open to view.

Illus. 54 gives a substantially different picture of pierced work. This stylized piece is strictly ornamental. Small blocks are fastened to its back so as to produce prominent shadows when hung and lighted against a wall. The oblique carving of sweeping curves contributes positively to the piece's attractiveness.

The ¾-inch pine used in the carving has been fashioned to create a sense of depth in some parts, and the base of the tree has been somewhat realistically detailed to avoid mistaking the subject for something else. Other parts have been more radically simulated. Space arrangement was a major, if not the main, matter of concern in design. Balance, contrast, and unity also had to be adequately taken into account.

Producing Effective Results

Although relief carving has many possibilities and few limitations, the result remains the basis of verdict. Relevant conditions and influences, both aesthetic and technical, can affect an outcome. The factors to observe are:

• *Materials and Tools.* Limitations of available wood—its species, size, color, dryness, and grain structure—as well as the quality and variety of tools on hand can affect the carving.

• *Artistic Skill.* Limitations in design are realized according to the designer's imagination, creativity, and knowledge of the various aspects of the art.

• *External Forces.* Results may be influenced or controlled at the design stage by the demand of a client for a specific design, by cultural preferences about style, or by pressures from other outside sources.

• *Purpose of the Design.* Shape may be significantly modified if the carving is to be an ornament which matches an existing decor or if it is to be made for a particular use.

• *Carving Skill.* Results depend to a great extent also on the carver's ability to produce as intended, his patience, his knowledge of carving, his ability to visualize results, and even his physical environment.

The importance of design in the scheme of things should not be minimized. Not only must the designer have knowledge of design principles and rules but also his repertoire must include knowledge of the techniques of carving. Only through an awareness of the limitations and potentialities of the different kinds of carving can he adequately anticipate results. The level of expertise he achieves will grow in relation to his ability to mesh the technical requirements and the important considerations of design.

In the beginning, the designer should learn to develop designs along the lines of the styles depicted in Illus. 55. He should become skilled enough to create several forms of an object within a style of his preference, while producing work fitting for the purpose at hand. The two conventionalized arrangements shown relate to this point. The formalized arrangement at (A) would suit nicely along a center-line of a symmetrically balanced piece of furniture. The one at (B) would be more appropriately placed in a right-angled corner, especially if it counterbalances something in an opposite position. Careful application of these restrictions is necessary. Certain styles of design, as with the different kinds of woodcarving, are more suitable in some places than in others.

Decisions about quantity can be difficult, as well. Knowing how broad, how deep, or how bold a carving should be for a project poses a serious challenge, and judging when enough is enough is one of the most difficult things for a craftsman to learn. The tendency to overdecorate should be avoided, especially since comparatively plain decorations are preferred today.

Carvings of extraordinarily elaborate design are sometimes produced in relief. Such work often shows great skill in the handling of tools, as with a floral design in which the leaves and petals have been severely undercut to the delicate thickness of the living plant. Carving of that kind requires skill of unquestioned degree, but by no means could it be applied to a project subject to handling. Even the mere touching of the thinly shaped wood could result in breakage and ruin. Some woodcarvers are evidently overcome by an urge to show an exceptional ability at the expense of practicality.

The craftsman must learn to judge what will be appropriate for a project. From a pragmatic point of view, his plan should bring together materials and methods which will result in a sufficiently substantial product. That, for all practical purposes, may be taken as a rule.

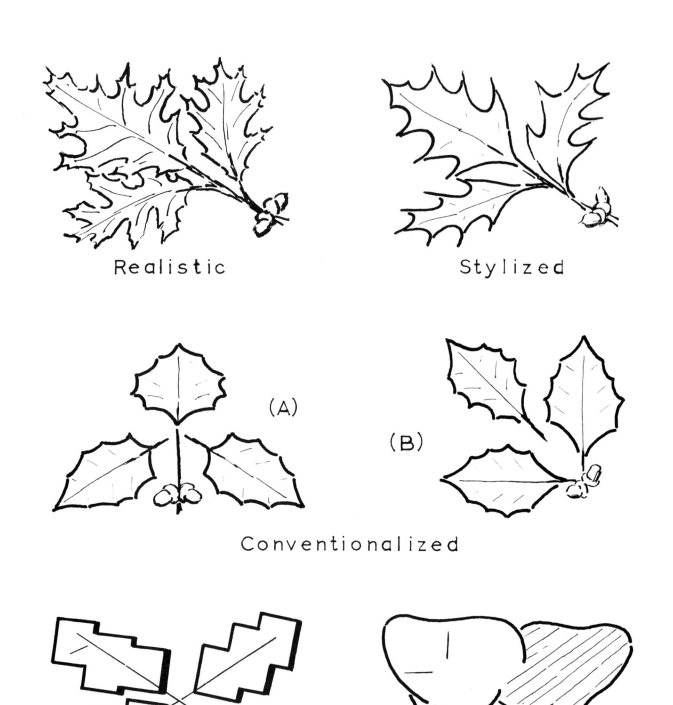

Realistic

Stylized

(A)

(B)

Conventionalized

Geometric

Abstract

Illus. 55. A skilled designer can modify forms to suit his purpose.

V
INCISED-
CARVING DESIGN

Carving by incising is a unique craft. It is almost relief carving in reverse, as cuts are taken entirely within an object's outline instead of around it, eliminating the need to carve a background. By the same token, wood left standing prohibits a precise representation of natural form. This limitation, though, seems to have done little to restrict the craft's development and originality over the years.

Learning from Past Practice

Over the years, the terms *hollow relief* and *sunken relief* came into use as identifiers of special kinds of carving. The terms aptly described methods involving incising which were perfected in earlier centuries. One method evolved in Egypt and the other in Italy.

The Egyptian form of carving was carried out by cutting along a design's outline with the tool held nearly perpendicular to the surface of the material. The edges of the subject were then rounded to a depth similar to that in shallow relief. Further incising of details added a bit of realism to the design. It was less work than other methods since much of the area within the incised outline remained flat and in the plane of the original surface. Today this is known as the

coelanaglyphic method. Illus. 56 and Illus. 57 show a modern application of this method. The decoration has an extraordinarily subtle effect on the lamp base with its bold pyramidal blocking. Since the features of this type of decoration are so sparingly incised, one can readily understand how the method became so popular among the ancients for recording their picture stories.

The stylized bird on the lamp has some significance besides the carving method. First of all, the design shows that nature does not always reveal itself symmetrically. Even in figures inherently bisymmetrical, another view may create a more interesting balance. Secondly, the special treatment of the shape balances a concave contour against one of convex curvature. The technique imparts a distinctly rhythmic quality to the figure. It is a technique worth remembering.

The second kind of carving mentioned, *intaglio*, represents a form of decorating which came into prominence in Italy. Intaglio and the Egyptian forms differ, although both leave the surface unaltered outside an object's outline. Intaglio reveals an object's image. The higher elevations of a figure or design are hollowed out deeply, actually in reverse of normal relief carving.

Intaglios are generally kept small. They sometimes are used to decorate glass and clear plastic containers, with the engraving done on the inside of some pieces. A design in a form of

Illus. 56. This lamp base was carved by a method developed in ancient Egypt.

Illus. 57. A close-up showing the powerful effect of counterbalancing concave and convex shapes in a figure.

intaglio decorates the walnut mail holder in Illus. 58, such that the design of the holly is shaped as if berries and the underside of leaves left impressions. Balance and variety are maintained by having placed the carvings in alternate positions. The project illustrates once again how effective a simple design can be on a project. It also demonstrates the common practice of keeping intaglios close to reality in size and shape.

Much of the furniture made in America before the turn of the century was embellished by hand-carving. Incised botanical decorations became quite prevalent. Although pussy willow and wheat designs emerged as particularly pleasing forms, some of the outlined figures were less appealing to the trained eye. Oftentimes a single flower stalk was carved with dissimilar sets of flowers and leaves attached. The appeal of the work has grown over the years (as is evident in antique shops), with the more carefully hand-crafted pieces leading the demand.

Designs of the period were incised principally in stylized form. Several have been reproduced in Illus. 54. They were adapted from decorations used in nineteenth-century cabinetry. A modernized version of an old arrangement has been applied in the design of the letter holder in Illus. 60.

Developing a Contemporary Style

The stylized method of designing continues to gain acceptance. A reason for its rising popularity

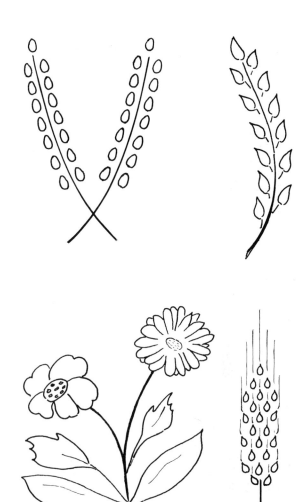

Illus. 58. Decorations requiring little depth can be given a realistic appearance by carving them in the form of intaglio.

Illus. 59 (above right). Various designs, including mixed flowers, were often incised on 19th-century cabinets.

Illus. 60 (right). A letter holder incised in a modified version of a carving done some time before the turn of the century.

becomes apparent as one considers the sources of design and the manner in which they can be adapted. Plants and animals are the usual subjects, but the designs need not be made to look like restricted interpretations of the natural forms. The method allows for modification to any degree desired. In that way, the designer has an opportunity to impart a personal touch to his decorations.

As in relief carving, a design for incising must be suitable for the wood. Depth of cut is an obvious consideration. Since most wood for project construction has a nominal thickness of an inch or less, not just any method of carving will do for the large figures. In some places, an incised carving will do if the full depth or background of a relief carving cannot be accommodated satisfactorily.

In applications of one kind, the woodcarver traces around the pencilled outline. It seems the easiest carving of all, but, in reality, it is somewhat difficult. Maintaining uniform grooves presents the biggest challenge. Machine routing could help, if a way can be devised to assure the smoothness and regularity of curves. Attempts to correct unwanted waviness in a line invariably affect appearance. Because of this, designs outlined by routing are often used in the mechanically controlled duplications of mass production.

Generally, the mechanistic quality of outlined designs can be avoided by incising nongeometrical forms and figures. When developing a scene, for instance, an interesting effect can be produced by varying the depth and width of cuts within and about the edges of figures. An uncommon variation of this kind decorates the hard-

Illus. 61. A record chest with interesting and uniquely outlined shapes in a stylization of a scene.

Illus. 62. Variations for effect and emphasis were produced by altering the depth and width of incisions.

wood chest in Illus. 61 and Illus. 62. The practice of shaping about an outline with a narrow gouge or veiner produces the result seen in the horizon in the scene. The birds, by contrast, show the results of carving with flat and V-shaped tools. A carefully controlled knife blade suffices for the thin components. A more realistic representation could not be obtained by the incised method of carving.

As to composition, the components of the design are totally stylized. The birds represent swift flyers of no particular species, with the dynamic thrust of illustrated flight counterbalanced by the apparent stability of distant mountains. Differences in size, position, and direction prevail as if the members of the flock were making quick maneuvres of avoidance. The openness of the composition simulates the spaciousness of the sky and surrounding areas. Placed for normal viewing from above, the composition presents a comparatively large surface near the top in order to maintain the desired sense of unobstructed space.

The stylized manner of designing produces interesting effects in other ways, especially when cuts are suggestive of detail. The technique is most useful for details which are repetitive and more numerous than can be advantageously incised. The spread-out, imbricated parts of a pine cone are a good example. Pine needles are handled similarly in many applications.

Incising requires special ability. Narrow,

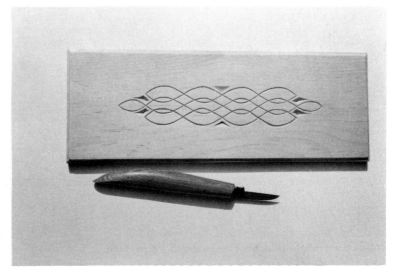

Illus. 63. Some formalized patterns, as on the lid of a pen and pencil box, may be given the delicate appearance that narrowly incised lines provide.

smooth, and sharply made incisions are customary requirements. A knife with a well-honed and pointed blade will do. Also, the adeptness of the carver to produce precisely as intended should be known to the designer (if the two are not the same person). A limited ability on the part of the carver could leave the designer's intentions far from being fulfiled.

The carving on the box lid in Illus. 63 demonstrates the importance of uniformly precise and delicately executed carving. While the formalized design holds no special meaning, it represents the kind of decoration appropriate for certain purposeful uses. Carefully done, the incised lines would serve beautifully on a box for holding items which also should be used with care and exactness. Poorly or crudely executed designs would defeat that purpose.

On occasion, designs are created in a manner having special significance for a particular person. Animals are familiar subjects. They usually are given a relationship to a name or event worthy of lasting memory. A meaning, humorous or serious, can be imparted by the clever stylization of shapes, as in Illus. 64.

The conventional designing style provides another sufficiently flexible means of authentically contemporary creations. Nonformalized compositions seem the least traditional option, and such arrangements as a straightforward, repetitive grouping of flower heads are capable of being arranged in a number of configurations. Designs of this type require proper positioning. The shallowly incised design in Illus. 65 conforms to these suggestions. Notice how the carving fits in without detracting from the function of

Illus. 64. Wood can be incised as a simplified stylization or to simulate details in a more realistic representation.

Illus. 65. Light from above emphasizes the contemporary formation of incised flowers.

the board. The light from above makes the flowers stand out in sharp detail. Illus. 66 shows some possibilities.

One can sense how easily the layout in Illus. 66 was incised. The repetitiveness of detail is why. Gouges were used to shape each petal, with a single cut or two usually doing the job. The main design problem is keeping the composition in balance.

Applying Geometric Methods

Geometric incising uses designs constructed with compass, ruler, and pencil. Carving in this style takes two forms: outline and solid-figure shaping. The latter, better known as *chip carving*, commonly involved the shaping of rosettes and other patterns which radiate from a center. Both forms of carving utilize fundamental elements of geometry, but their inspiration may also come from nature.

Outlined shapes are formed much like other styles. Gouged or V-cuts trace a border or other geometric shape in the plane of the surface. The incisions can follow any number of rectangular and curved configurations. Arcs, circles, S-

Illus. 66. The grouping of flowers in a unified manner is a conventionalization adaptable to surfaces of different shapes.

curves, rectangles, triangles, zigzags, and chevrons represent the many different components incorporated into fully formed geometric patterns.

Straight-lined cuts are equally popular. They are usually applied with a groove spaced slightly away from and closely parallel to the edge of the finished board's surface. Such decorations, though plain in form, often provide all the carving needed. Machine-routed grooves on drawer fronts of dressers are familiar examples. The work requires considerable precision, whether mechanically controlled or done by hand machining. Guiding the tool in a straight line becomes essential at times. Hand tooling affords no exception.

Illus. 67 includes some of the cuts possible by machine and hand tooling. In order to eliminate the rounded ends of the gouged or routed grooves, a flat-bladed skew or a fishtail serves nicely. Either way, the need to incise the geometric patterns uniformly and evenly is of extreme importance.

Illus. 67. Circular and straight cuts in outlined form.

Incising in the Abstract

While boredom from repetition remains an ever-present danger in geometric design, the very opposite possibility must be guarded against when designing in the abstract. Too much variety leaves the work without a unified appearance. To avoid this, a similarity of shapes, compactness of features, or an element which functions as a thread tying the separate parts together should be used. Combinations of these things often serve best.

The designing of incised abstractions follows essentially the same rules as abstractions intended for carving by other methods. The work must conform in matters of balance, mass, unity, and proportion. In addition, an abstraction may or may not represent a subject. It may be slightly, moderately, or severely styled, leaving the designer largely uninhibited to present a design any way he chooses.

With abstract incisions, the wood surrounding the decoration remains in view and imposes somewhat of a practical design limitation. Depth of cut imposes another. Still, incising gives the abstractionist ample leeway for creative expression. Almost any shape that can be outlined on paper can be made into a carving.

An abstract composition decorates the paper

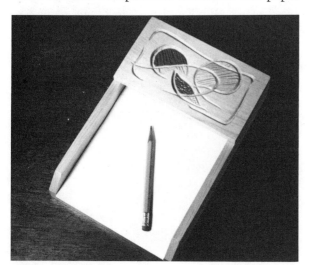

Illus. 68. Bright colors and texture bring the abstract representation of autumn leaves to life on this paper tray.

tray in Illus. 68. The gouged lines are an important element. They define the abstract leaves, keep the observer's eye moving among the different components, weave within and about the arrangement in a unifying manner, and add a bit of interest when shadows appear. By themselves, the lines would seem rhythmic but seriously dull. The texture of the leaves provides the needed variety, and the use of fall colors heightens interest. The leaves become more pronounced, while the gouged lines take on a subordinate role. A balance of attractions results.

Piercing by Incising

Piercing of wood by incising results in the complete removal of material within an outline, unlike piercing in relief where the figures take shape from the removal of wood in surrounding areas. In incised work, piercing produces a sense of beauty only insofar as the profiles themselves warrant it.

A design suitable for this method of carving must have a contour which will create sufficient visual interest. The pierced opening contrasts with the surface around it, and this feature alone must produce the necessary effect, since no other detail remains within the outline to complement it. For purposes of comparison, imagine producing an outstanding work of art in two-dimensional silhouette. Some desirable projects can be made by piercing, nonetheless.

In carving generally, and in piercing particularly, an added measure of significance results when the carving fulfils a practical purpose. A carving should always beautify wood wherever applied, but it will exhibit most meaning if it is designed according to some practical need. The floral design through the shell of the night light in Illus. 69 shows the idea. When placed in three or four locations, the lighted bulb will cast the design in enlarged pattern onto adjacent or near surfaces. It also helps if the design leaves a favorable impression in the light of day.

Keep in mind when making projects such as this to use, by all means, a bulb which gives off

Illus. 69. Conventionalized figures function very well on a night light when pierced at equal intervals.

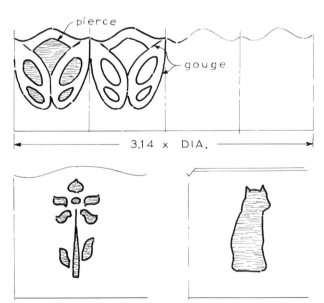

Illus. 70. A layout for a night light with alternate designs for piercing.

little heat. The type of bulb installed in Christmas-tree ornaments do best.

Another recommendation pertains not so much to safety, but to ease of construction. A considerable amount of difficult carving can be avoided by first boring the wood; then enlarging and shaping the cavities with a sharp blade (Illus. 70). Power equipment helps ease the especially difficult task of smoothing the large center opening.

Lettering Signs and Mottos

Some things may not be abstracted. The alphabet is one of them. It *must* meet the criterion of legibility, and that can be achieved only by maintaining recognizable letters. Without this continuity of form, the meaning and usefulness of the symbols will be seriously impaired.

By no means does the need for continuity imply that all lettering must be similar in style. Several different styles are familiar to nearly all readers. Moreover, words are sometimes extended, condensed, or italicized for effect. The best guideline for the person who wants to design his own lettering is to avoid an ornateness which impairs readability. Even the moderately embellished Old English style of lettering has only special uses.

Woodcarvers sooner or later become involved in carving letters. Whether done by incising or in relief, the limitations and rules must be known. The fundamentals are listed below. If they are studied in conjunction with a careful analysis of some printed lettering, the craftsman should be able to avoid careless errors and obtain some commendable results.

Uniformity—Evenness of height, proportion, inclination, and spacing must be maintained.

Proportion—In general, the ratio of a letter's height to its width is either 5:3 or 4:3. The exception is the letter *W*, which has a width equal to its height.

Spacing—Spacing between letters and between words is by area, not distance.

Stability—To avoid a top-heavy appearance, letters such as B and Z should have tops smaller than bottoms, and none of the letters should be given a horizontal stroke at mid-height. In the E it should be placed above mid-point; in the P and R, below.

Style—Letter styles (the capital and lower case forms) should not be mixed except when capitalizing words. Alphabetic styles, e.g., Roman and Gothic, should never be mixed in ordinary usage.

Legibility—Clarity must not be lost due to the distortion or excessive ornamentation of letters.

Good lettering results from both an artistic eye and careful execution. The woodcarver must be as skilful as the illustrator, for the finished lettering should have an appealing quality about it whether carved in wood or drawn on paper. The demands of design remain the same for both artist and craftsman.

The requirements apply when forming letters by hand or machine. Mechanically guided routers and sand-blasting techniques are frequently used. Both relief and incised lettering are produced, and both good and bad examples occur. Problems of sizing, spacing, and styling do not go away with power tools.

Illus. 72. Incised lettering, this in a form of modern Roman, stands out most vividly when the color of the surface contrasts with the grain revealed.

Illus. 71. An incised sign showing required information and a design inspired by the property's location.

Despite the possible advantage of machine work, the handcarving of letters still remains desirable. In fact, it may be superior where the preferred sizes and shapes of letters cannot be readily produced by other means. Mottos with small letters and folk-art signs are appropriately, if not necessarily, carved by hand.

In the lettering of property signs, both the letters and the signs can be given informational and symbolic meaning. The incised carving of the redwood sign in Illus. 71 meets a local requirement by identifying ownership and location in a clearly straight-forward manner. Other features have a different purpose. The sign's shape, the silver color, and the slant of the letters emphasize a relationship with the location of the lakeside property. Slanted lettering, in contrast to the vertical type, is somewhat more indicative of horizontal movement.

Modern Roman vertical lettering takes shape on the sign in Illus 72. The layout requires proper care. Concerns about uniformity, spacing, and proportion are as important as before.

When preparing to incise lettering, thought should be directed to contrast. A difference in color between the internal and external grain of the wood will give the letters prominence. A light wash of acrylic paint or thin coat of stain prior to carving will often produce the desired result on pieces lacking the contrast of aged wood. The choice of color, if any is to be added, may depend on whether or not the incised piece will be placed so that artificial light produces shadows in the letters.

Reviewing Applications

The constancy with which art impinges upon woodcarving may not be evident, but the basic principles cannot be avoided at any level of development in the craft. Neither the purpose nor complexity of carving minimizes the need to know those principles.

The individual who has acquired a working knowledge of design and has learned the methods by which the different styles can be carved is on the way to a complete understanding of woodcarving. He knows the bounds of the craft and realizes how much unlike the natural object his completed version will be. His work reflects, when desired, an ability to design around the more rigidly formalized geometric and conventional interpretations. Armed with enough knowledge, he can develop a distinctively personal kind of expression within the context of artistic design. In short, he can create a style of his own.

To help in gaining an understanding of woodcarving design, the reader might go back over the previously illustrated incised and relief carvings and analyze each one in a systematic way. Keep in mind in so doing that the large majority of carvings shown this far are for decorative purposes entirely. Not many of them serve another function.

Note the presence of balance, contrast, unity, rhythm, proportion, and repetition in the review. Determine, also, whether a design falls within the realistic, stylized, conventional, geometric, or abstract classification of style.

Other points to consider are if the design offers a balance of visual emphases and attractions, or does one part seem to stand out too conspicuously. Elements should be harmonious and complementary, lines arranged so they lead the eye smoothly in transition from one point to another, and the motif should unify through the spacing and similarity of forms. The other shapes should contain the variety needed to offset a feeling of monotony. These are some of the key thoughts about decorative work.

VI
CHIP CARVING
VARIATIONS

More often than not, conversations about incising lead to the topic of chip carving. Knowledgeable practitioners are especially fond of the method. Undoubtedly, many woodcarvers choose it for ease of application.

Repetition contributes to the appeal. Regularly repeated accents have compelling power. The repeated patterns may be simple or complex, and they may extend linearly or multidimensionally. The recurrence of attractive accents produces a rhythmic appearance when alternately or sequentially placed. An alternate placement of parts may involve size (large, small, large, small, and so on) while the use of sequential progressions of size may range from small to large in several degrees. The craftsman must remain alert to the potentials and the drawbacks inherent in designing by repetition.

Distinguishing Types

Chip carving entails removing geometric pieces of wood. There are variations. Segments of a cylinder, parts in the shape of wedges, and pyramid-like cavities having three sides define the basic figures. The three-sided cuts may have one or two of the sides positioned perpendicular to the wood's surface as an alternative to the common method of sloping all cuts to remove a chip. Either way, the grouped arrangements produce a strongly unified appearance.

The difference between chip carving and the other methods of incising comes about mostly from carving designs adapted for the different tools. Incising, by and large, makes use of tools with straight and curved tips, but chip carving is done exclusively with flat blades. Chip carvers use skew and square-nosed chisels or sharply pointed knife blades according to individual preferences. The results are practically the same.

Cuts made when chip carving create planar surfaces—flat, curved, or warped—depending on the design requirement and skill of the craftsman in using flat-bladed tools. Incising by gouging, by way of contrast, seldom produces a flat plane. The sectioned drawings in Illus. 73 reveal the difference.

Patterns for chip carving seem to flow from a designer's hand in endless diversity. Illus. 74 shows several possibilities. All are decorative forms of carving. They are applicable to surfaces all over, along borders, and in other selected spots. They can take the form of rosettes in radial layout, leaves or flowers in linear repetition, diamond and basket-weave patterns in over-all arrangement, or triangular and wedge-shaped figures for border-like application. By and large, the applications are geometric in nature.

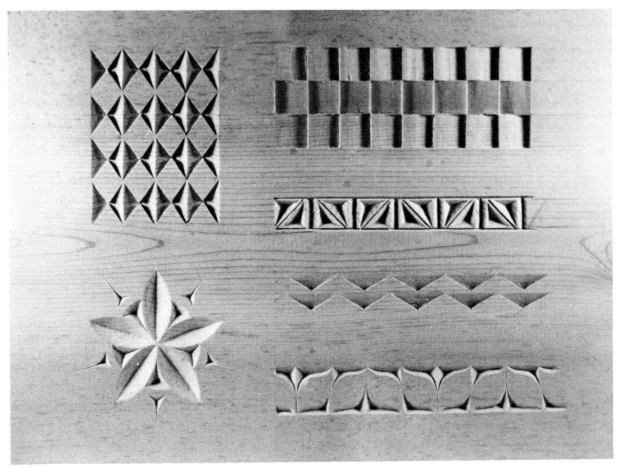

Illus. 73. Drawings for chip carving (top) and incising by gouging (bottom) point up the relationship of design to tooling.

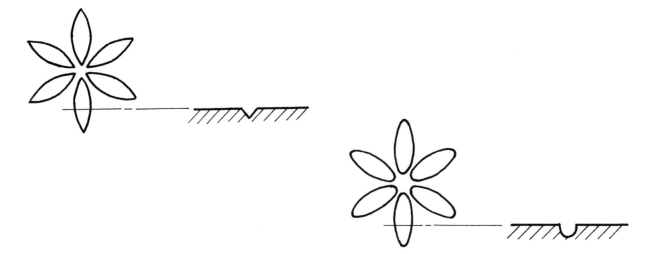

Illus. 74. The patterns on this sample board show the diversity possible by chip carving.

Designing Geometrically

By their very nature, planar cuts are geometric. Single units in a side-by-side arrangement make up a geometric pattern, in addition to the element of geometry contained within each unitary figure. The cuts can be combined in linear, circular, and radial formations.

Similar-sized triangular units are often combined in decorations for wooden projects. Their sharp edges require the accuracy in development that would be expected of the woodcarver. A carefully used measuring device with a straight edge becomes essential, and a plastic triangle, due to its transparency, allows for ease in layout. Given an accurate layout, the desired precision is more likely to result. Illus. 75 and Illus. 76 illustrate basic steps in the procedure.

Sharply, uniformly, and deeply incised carvings are the most appealing. Poor construction will make the sizing of parts difficult; carvings too shallow will not show the depth of shadow line which gives chip carving that extra measure of appeal; and a flatness or roundness at the intersection of sloping cuts where there should be a sharpness leaves a lacklustre dullness of detail. While these are important concerns for the woodcarver, none of his efforts will compensate for a poor design.

Geometric designs, perhaps more readily than other styles, can develop into overbearing embellishments. The designer must avoid the danger of both overadornment and repetitively monotonous patterns. The repetitiveness of like shapes bunched together becomes tiresome to view unless a detail is altered within the assembly, and a single, minor change will usually make

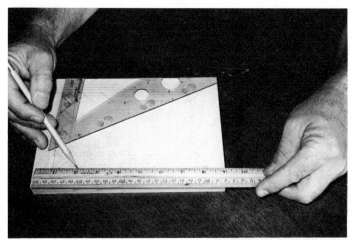

Illus. 75. A plastic triangle and a ruler are useful items when constructing patterns having straight lines.

Illus. 76. An accurate and carefully designed layout helps assure the desired result.

a big difference. Oftentimes the modification of a central point will suffice.

A carving with a modified cell among a series of triangles is seen in Illus. 77. The central design element is effective not because it represents anything in particular, but from showing curvature among straight-sided units. This is a technique well worth remembering.

The technical term for a pattern in which the units have parts in common with adjacent ones is *diaper*. Diaper work exhibits considerable solidarity and continuity. Geometrically carved designs customarily display these characteristics. The strength and uniqueness of the designs derive, for the most part, from the unified effect of repetition and from the variation of a figure within a group.

Patterns for chip carving can be readily adapted to other geometric shapes. Illus. 78 shows designs for different applications. Whether created by straight lines or arcs, the figures will sometimes be most interesting if an element within is left in the flat. The shaded sections of A and D should be left that way. The other designs made with interlocking circles may be carved with or without flat areas. When developing such figures, the possibilities seem limited only by the designer's ability and imagination.

Illus. 77. A single detail of different design is often sufficient to offset the monotonous effect of repeated geometric shapes.

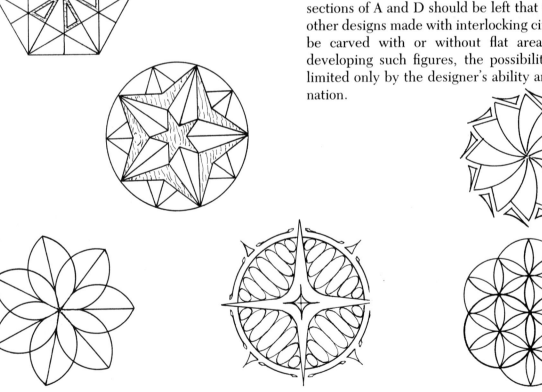

Illus. 78. Patterns for chip carving can be constructed in extensive variety with a few drawing instruments.

Dividing Geometric Forms

Success in chip carving depends to an extent on skill in constructing geometric figures and dividing circles into equal parts. For applications in linear design, the craftsman must be able to draw triangles of equal dimension, and he must be able to divide lines and areas into specific numbers of parts. Persons unable to handle a compass, ruler, and triangles sufficiently well for such basic procedures as erecting perpendiculars and drawing the simple polygons should consult a draftsman's text. In all probability, the person who cannot gain command of those basics will never develop the degree of competence needed.

Squares, hexagons, and octagons are easily constructed. They may be drawn either with a triangle and a T-square or by dividing circles into parts for locating corner points. Designs are usually developed directly on the wood, except for key points of complicated shapes, which are better transferred to the surface from paper.

Some constructions present more of a challenge than others, such as dividing circles into an odd number of parts. An easy (but time-consuming) method involves stepping off the perimeter with a dividers in a trial-and-error approach. The methods of applied geometry are effective but a bit more complicated.

Once divided into the required number of sections, the perimeter can be connected at the points with straight lines or arcs. One unit may be built upon another to create a design. An application based on the circle is carried into construction in Illus. 79-81.

Illus. 79. The center point must be precisely located for constructing a geometric design on a round piece.

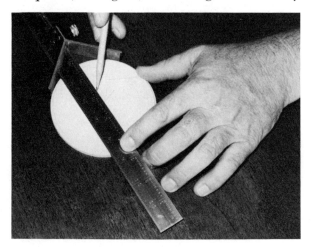

Illus. 80. Circular patterns in considerable variety can be developed with a compass.

Illus. 81 (left). *A specially made bench hook with a V-notch helps control round stock during the carving operation.*

Illus. 82 (below). *The incising of a floral design with flat-bladed tools produces an unusual visual effect.*

Any species of wood that can be carved by other methods may be used, but those having a straight grain and relatively plain texture serve best. Ease in carving is one thing. The appearance of the pattern is the other.

Drawing from Nature

Besides geometry, inspiration may come from nature. Chip carving will not result in a facsimile of a natural object, but it can combine planar cuts in recognizable natural form. Flowers seem to be particularly adaptable to this method.

The note box in Illus. 82 contains such a design. Several points about the carving should be observed, particularly the comparatively simple form, its placement, the arrangement, and the rather unusual manner in which the geometric cuts have been made to create the figure. Although another design or method of carving would do as well, the product as finished is entirely appropriate for the purpose.

Floral designs can be created which appear less geometric than most while making use of the chip-carving technique. Illus. 83 shows a sketch of this type. As before, the design is incised with a flat blade. Even though such shapes are more difficult to carve than those with straight lines, the decorative effect achieved in the product makes the effort worthwhile.

Chip-carved petals in a straight-lined design will be three-sided, whereas those outlined in curves will have two sides. The freehand shapes in Illus. 83 may require a paring action in order to complete each V-cut. The curved petals and leaves are most easily carved with a knife or a bent square-nosed chisel. Where sides of parts merge, enough wood must be removed to form a sharp parting line but not so much that the edge falls below the flat surface.

Illus. 83. Floral designs may be given a geometric form (right) or a less-structured shape.

A similar recommendation applies when carving the design in Illus. 84. From this example, one gains a broader sense of the kinds of shapes produceable by chip carving. The gradual variations in depth of incising and the transitional sweep of the outline leads the eye in pleasant movement.

Being Selective

An important consideration in design is whether or not an object will be better with a carved decoration than without one. If carving is warranted, then what and how much? A designer's work should always be reviewed in this context.

Compared to many traditional applications, the designs in this text generally have a quality of simplicity about them. They do not fill all visible areas. That fact contrasts markedly with objects customarily carved in primitive style. There are times when no carving at all would be preferable to a conglomeration of minutely incised details. The practice of placing details everywhere about an article not only hides the grain and natural beauty of the wood, but also eliminates the powerful effect of an incised pattern contingent to a plain area. Selectivity of use should always outweigh displays of unconstrained skill in carv-

Illus. 84. A layout of a motto-board designed for deep incising.

73

ing. No amount of carving, regardless of how expertly done, will substitute for an inelaborate design of high quality.

Being selective in chip carving is highly important. The opportunities for artistic expression are so favorable that the urge to decorate without restraint must be kept under control. A designer who applies the patterns sparingly will be more likely to produce outstanding work, and a good one will not engage in the uncontrolled mixing of shapes. Unrestrained carving inevitably leads to incongruous forms of embellishment.

A sound practice is to keep designs comparatively plain, while avoiding the tendency to adorn all visible space. The greater the detail the more likely the introduction of inharmonious elements. Quality aside, the sheer burden of quantity of geometric decoration could be an irremediable detraction. Occasionally, a piece will be observed which has so much detail that the trained eye remains unmoved by the artless mixture in an otherwise superb carving.

Illus. 85 may be viewed in this context. If the design has a fault, it certainly is not over-embellishment. The carving method used is not nearly as meaningful a consideration as are concerns about size, uniformity, and placement of the design.

The carefully arranged details on this coin bank invite the proper amount of attention. They overcome the austerity of total plainness. Further interest is directed to the piece by the coloring, both for purposes of contrast and to hide the glued-up sections of the hollow article. Paint improved the appearance considerably.

An indication of the artistic merit of a design may be gained by considering whether the carving seems overbearing or an effective enhancement. The viewer, upon taking in all features of the article, should feel good about what he sees. His concentration can then be directed to the specific principles of design involved. The problem for the craftsman, of course, is to make those determinations before beginning to carve.

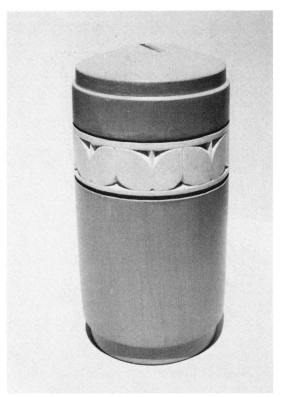

Illus. 85. The V-cutting characteristic of chip carving produces a striking effect on cylindrical surfaces when carefully executed.

VII
WHITTLED AND SCULPTURED FORMS

Whittling—a method of shaping figures in the round—remains the most popular form of woodcarving. One reason why relates to the relative ease with which designs can be produced. Another is its long standing as a leisure-time activity.

Carving wood in the shape of a known object does not present some of the major problems encountered in relief and incised work. Figures are more easily detailed when made as we are accustomed to viewing them. There is no need to contend with the restrictions of an attached background, lack of depth, or perspective. Furthermore, a carving intended for full three-dimensional shaping can be made without any consideration whatsoever to fitting it to a project or a surrounding area, and only several of the rules borrowed from two-dimensional art need be considered when designing carvings of this type.

Preferences of individuals interested in woodcarving frequently center on practices which involve the least difficulty. The wood must be easy to move, hold, and carve. That way a person can take a rough piece to a place where he can sit and rest, position the work by hand, and casually do the shaping with a single blade. Only when whittling small pieces are such practices entirely possible. Other carvings generally require several tools and some form of clamping. Although not all pieces can be handled in the leisurely manner portrayed here, the results achieved may be little different from those obtained under more rigorous conditions.

The procedure for carving in the round customarily begins with a two-view drawing, as in Illus. 86. Full-size views are needed if the contours are to be traced onto the wood (Illus. 87). The excess wood may then be removed from around the object's outline by whatever means the craftsman has available (Illus. 88). Final shaping of the figure proceeds according to the size of the piece and the hardness of the wood (Illus. 88).

Illus. 86. Two-view sketches generally suffice for carving in the round.

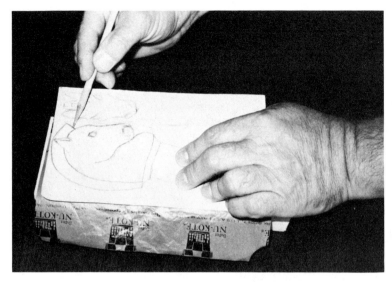

Illus. 87 (above). Producing the object's profile on the wood is basic in carving.

Illus. 88 (right). Removing as much excess wood as practical by sawing makes the carving easier.

Illus. 89 (below). Objects carved by whittling are usually hand-held during the process.

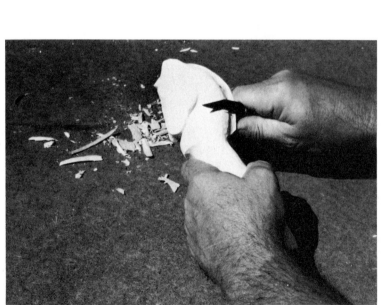

Observing Practical Differences

The question ultimately arises as to whether carving wood in the round is whittling or sculpturing. At the risk of seeming facetious, the difference may be merely a matter of attitude. More likely, it hinges on a number of considerations, including the tools, the artistry, and the nature of the carving involved.

By definition, whittling has to do with the paring of wood or removal of chips using a knife. Sculpturing, on the other hand, refers to the use of any tool for chiseling, cutting, gouging, chipping, or abrading a material to shape. In that sense, there occurs a difference in the mechanics of the process. Sculptures are seldom made with a knife alone (Illus. 90–92).

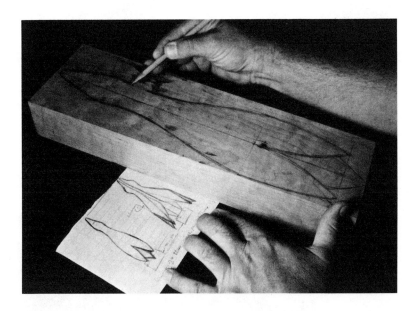

Illus. 90. An outline may also be sketched directly on the wood after the design has been worked out on paper.

Illus. 91. Power sawing is most welcome, even by craftsmen strictly committed to traditional methods of carving.

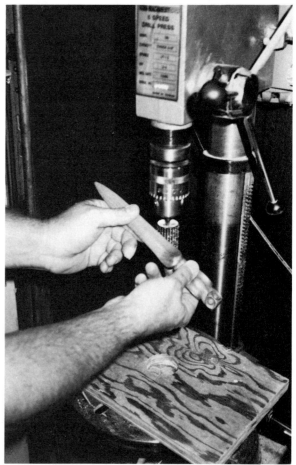

Illus. 92. A mallet, chisels, and bench hold are necessary in the hand sculpturing of a firm wood such as cherry.

Illus. 93. Use of a spindle rasp in a drill press helps at times when shaping extremely hard pieces of wood.

The level of artistic expression is a second difference. Comparing whittling with sculpting is analogous to contrasting the musical tones produced by a fiddler and those of a concert violinist. The musicians play in a similar manner, but the violinist brings the result to a higher state of art. Would the whittler's work then be rough textured and the sculptor's polished smooth? Not necessarily. But a virtuoso's work will likely stand out in any case.

This implies a third difference: that distinguishable qualities of subjects are present. In this view, some forms of design are more appropriate for one method of carving than for the other. The cruder pocketknife creations are likely to be considered folk art, while abstract carvings are more often associated with serious art. Caricatures are normally made by whittling soft wood, and highly dramatic pieces usually take form when sculpturing the firmer species. These thoughts have merit when designing. The larger the selection of tools used, the greater the opportunities to attain the required level of refinement. Taken altogether—tools, subjects, and distinctiveness of construction—the several factors provide a good idea of the difference between the two methods.

Whittling and sculpturing actually have more similarities than differences. Both begin with a design that is traced or drawn onto wood, and the shapes are then roughed out by sawing. The similarities in the procedures are pointed up in Illus. 89 and Illus. 92.

The sculpturing of hard woods requires a good physical setting. A solid bench with vise and clamping devices is a minimum. One should also have an adjustable bench stop.

Power tools have a practical purpose, as well. Many varieties can be had, most of which serve adequately when roughing the wood. One variety, the rotary rasp, makes necessary the manipulation of the wood rather than the tool when used in a drill press (Illus. 93).

Craftsmen steeped in tradition may abhor the use of power tools even for rough shaping, but those of a more pragmatic mind will utilize any development which eases the work preparatory to the final shaping. Whatever the personal conviction, the product lasts a while and makes the impression. The process fades quickly from view.

Carving Animal Figures

Except for certain abstract applications, preferences of subject are much the same among whittlers and sculptors. Without a doubt, designs of subjects for carving in the round are comprised mostly of human beings and animals. People seem to have an affinity for those forms in their different moods and postures. Then, too, the figures require no background for support as in the carving of delicate flowers. Large figures can also be scaled down effectively. They are reducible to nearly any size desired while retaining much of the appeal of the original. Flexibility of that magnitude may well be the main reason for the popularity of those figures.

Since whittling and sculpturing are special forms of three-dimensional art, mass and appurtenant space become the predominant characteristics. Line, which defines shape, and shape, which defines contour, are frequently minimized. Surface texture, likewise, ordinarily has a more subordinate part.

The effectiveness of the design of solid figures depends mostly on the distribution of mass. The designer must learn to proportion it so that an object will not be top heavy or seem out of balance. Angling a figure to give it an appearance of motion is another consideration. Both have a dynamic effect. Docility, serenity, and placidity are among the possibilities in a stationary portrayal. The skill with which these matters are handled will determine the quality of the outcome.

Style continues to be a principal concern for the designer. The opportunities for interpretation that go along with the five possible styles make figure carving a highly interesting part of the craft.

In Illus. 94, a realistic carving of the American bison is shown as fashioned from pine wood and

Illus. 94. Dark stain applied to the white pine imparts more of a realistic appearance to this bison.

Illus. 95. The realistic appearance of a carving can also be enhanced with acrylics and parts as naturally grown.

stained. The sealed-in dark stain imparts a much more natural appearance to the bison than the white pine alone would have produced. It also accents the parts carved to represent woolly hair on the head and shoulders. Tufts of dried grass, first glued to the base and then tinted green, lend an interesting touch of reality to the arrangement. The carving itself is small, giving evidence of how a large animal can be scaled to fit a piece of wood 2 x 3½ x 6 inches over-all.

The squirrel in Illus. 95 has about the same dimensions as the bison. It, too, resembles a natural model. The oak base and the acorns in the arrangement are real, but the acrylic paints and part on which the squirrel balances are, of course, simulated. Although the grey paint hides a defect in the wood, it does not show the animal's hair tips as would be done in a precise imitation. Much of the realistic appearance comes about by having given the figure a familiar posture and careful detailing about the eyes.

The use of items from nature has a marked effect in an arrangement. The bark section effectively adds to the squirrel model, as does fine grass on the bison. Such techniques are used to greatest advantage in realistic displays.

When making a stylized interpretation, the designer should be concerned primarily with matters other than the special effects derived from using natural items. The design should stress a characteristic of the object, and should not incorporate anything of natural form (except, of course, for the wood). His main purpose is interpretation rather than replication.

Illus. 96 represents the kind of design in which only slightly distorted features are desired. This manner of stylization captures the special effect intended. The facial expression makes the point. (When carving the piece, using a power tool as in Illus. 97 aids substantially in removing wood from behind the feline's "twitching" tail.)

All degrees of stylization are expressions in which one or more parts of an object undergo modification for purposes of emphasis. The subject, however, always remains clearly identifiable. The distortion may be in the mood, in a peculiar physical feature, or in several such things combined. The finished work may be humorous or entirely serious.

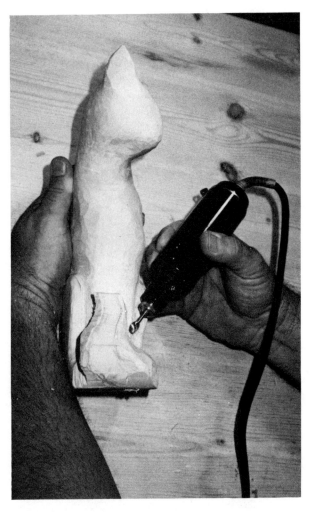

Illus. 97. Power carving with a rotary bit is especially useful in difficult-to-reach places.

Illus. 98 displays woodcarvings in which a feature has been much more radically altered than that in the previous example. The subjects are called "Sophisti-cats." Having been carved in redwood and finished in the natural, their smooth surfaces help to direct attention to aspects of form.

The kittens in the photograph are much the same as the cat, except for size. They have identical postures, shapes, proportions and color. The extensive elongation and the posture stress a feline's neck-stretching curiosity. The grain of the wood shows up as a difference in the litter, and the positions within the group are a way of providing variety in the assembly.

In a study of the shapes, one profile may normally have more appeal than the next. A preference could result from an individual's inclination towards the solid positioning of symmetrical shape or for the lines of an asymmetrical contour. Whatever the choice, Illus. 98 shows only two of the many positions which could be presented. Symmetry appears when viewing balanced shapes along the lines of a single plane dividing the form into similar halves. All other views present an asymmetrical configuration. Some profiles are especially attractive for leading the line of sight in a gradual sweep of seemingly rhythmic quality. It is this feature in the design of animals from which whittling and sculpturing derive much of their variety, interest, and appeal.

Some carvings of animals may be made even more abstract than the stylized versions. Realistic features may be almost totally absent, with barely a hint of the source inspiring the design. Illus. 99 illustrates the type. The piece exemplifies the importance of mass and space in sculpturing.

The arrangement of the birds in rapid descent has been designed for viewing from any of several angles. That fact made the planning a major challenge. Maintaining a visual balance among the parts was most difficult.

To give the design a smoothness to indicate the tight feathering of gliding birds, the walnut figures were carved to shape with a high-speed

Illus. 98. This stylization of felines emphasizes their natural curiosity.

cutting tool and polished by hand sanding. Depth was produced by connecting the elements with short rods. Two coats of satin polyurethane finished the sculpture.

The idea of the design is to instill in the viewer a sense of gliding motion in a unified and balanced grouping. A little experience observing birds in flight and an active imagination are needed for a full appreciation of the piece. Abstract modifications of this kind, whether retaining recognizable details or not, always excite the imaginations of some observers more than others.

Many birds are so graceful of form and movement that they have become favorite subjects among woodcarvers. Some craftsmen concentrate exclusively on the carving of wildfowl. They fashion the creatures more frequently in natural-

Illus. 99. These boldly represented birds in descending flight were sculptured in walnut with power tools.

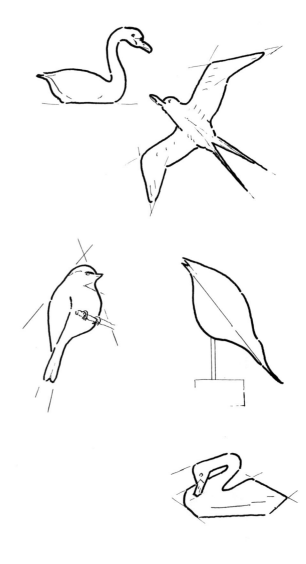

istic style than in others, and they collectively copy almost all of the positions presented in nature.

Several possibilities are suggested in Illus. 100. The range of implied styling extends from the realistic to the abstract. The identity of the birds remains evident, even in the most streamlined of the sketches.

When representing an animal in a streamlined abstraction, a carefully executed design will concentrate on a thought or attitude. A heron seeking prey and · a ground squirrel in an erect position as on the lookout for danger are two suggestions. The skills of both designer and carver come to bear in the modification of natural form.

Illus. 100. Birds are favorite subjects for woodcarving, due to their graceful qualities and the many possibilities for expression.

83

Modifying Form

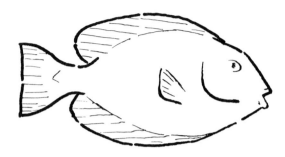

The person who can modify form opens a world of opportunities. He may select a single style, or he may wish to apply his talent to the several styles. The only real stipulation is to follow acceptable procedures for sketching and designing.

As a beginning point, a person planning to carve some form of animal should make a sketch of the creature. A realistic outline will suffice initially; then, if the carver wishes, he can proceed with a less lifelike representation by sketching in alterations of the features to be emphasized. In lieu of a specific emphasis, he may simply desire to create a general likeness. Small carvings must often be made that way. Carvings in miniature cannot be given the exactness of real figures (Illus. 101). Any provision to be made for finishing a carving should be taken into account during the design process.

Abstract

pin clasp

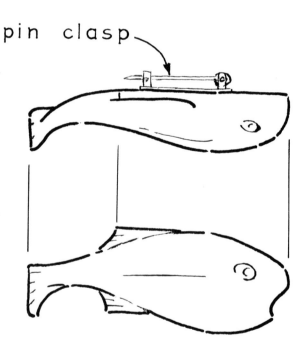

Illus. 101. Form takes on greater importance as size and detail diminish.

Modifications of natural form in three styles are shown in Illus. 102. The shapes are limited somewhat by their intended purpose as brooches. The backs of the carvings are flat, and no easily broken projections are included.

Illus. 102. Modifications of natural form designed for carving as brooches or overlays.

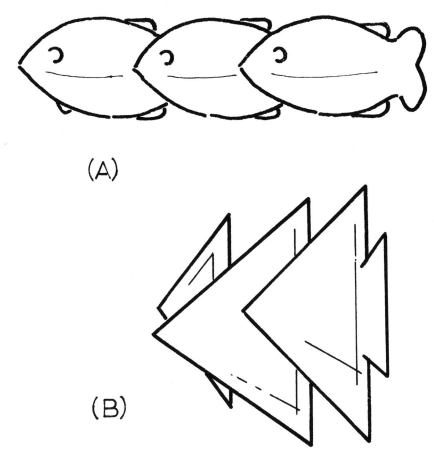

Illus. 103. Representations of fish in (A) conventionalized and (B) geometric configurations.

Similar applications are possible in the conventional and geometric styles, with their customary repetitiveness or forced configuration. Either way, the subject must conform accordingly. The designer should turn to any type that allows for greatest freedom of expression.

In keeping with the previous drawing, applications with fish as the subject are used in Illus. 103. The first repeats form in a conventional configuration. The second represents a small school done geometrically. An indication of the variations attainable by these formalized methods may be gained by studying the shapes.

When dealing with the human figure, work done in the past has significance for the designer.

Statuary in designs familiar to nearly everyone have stood through the ages. They have survived because of the durable materials from which sculptured, but an occasional wooden piece has been preserved in displayable condition. Of relatively recent origin, wooden figures of American Indians in feathered headdress have graced the entrances of cigar stores, and small carvings of horse attendants in the pre-automotive era were securely placed for use as hitching posts. Much of the carving of humans from wood in modern times has been done in a humorous vein or in caricature. The more serious of the works have been cast in bronze. Wood lacks the durability required for outside displays.

Whittling Caricatures

The caricature exaggerates some peculiarity or condition, being given a whimsical, humorous, or more or less ridiculous flair. The carving of such expressions requires special care. An upturned corner of the mouth could represent glee, happiness, amusement, smugness, or contempt, depending on subtle changes in facial treatment. Radical distortions are often used for overstatement.

A highly stylized whittling has severely distorted features. The practice of providing human beings with enlarged noses, ears, thumbs, and toes is common. Other parts of the anatomy may be similarly carved out of proportion. A round belly, twisted face, or elongated torso afford additional opportunities.

The stylization of caricatures derives some of its popularity from the fact that precise proportions need not be maintained. For example, a poorly sized anatomical limb could be a humorous modification. Because of the desirability of distortion, caricaturing and stylizing go hand in hand. Few combinations of style and design representation occur in equally complementary fashion.

When creating a caricature, a theme or manner of expression must be kept in mind. An

Illus. 104. "Instant of Towline Failure" is an appropriate title for this caricature whittled in basswood for a water-skiing enthusiast.

emotion, whether customary or unusual, could be the main emphasis. Additionally, the subject should be something of interest to the person for whom the object will be made.

In Illus. 104 a caricature is presented that seems to appeal most to persons familiar with water skiing. The humor stems from the character himself and the situation of momentary towline failure. The backward leaning position and stoutness of legs stress the posture and muscularity of an obviously accomplished skier, while the smugness of accomplishment on his face seems about to disappear as his eyes widen in realization of the moment upon him. As should be the case in any effective caricature, a certain amount of believability is carried forth by having maintained a semblance of reality.

Aside from the general shapes of body and skis, the assembly acquires credibility from the use of colors. A yellow cord represents the broken towline. The color of the body, a deep tan, is actually the natural tone of the basswood with a clear finish. The textured brown on the swimming trunks shows an effect obtained with a wood-burning tool (Illus. 105), and acrylic paints sparingly shade the hair, eyes, and foot straps.

Two additional points need to be mentioned. The first re-emphasizes the need to work out the design on paper, even if the outline will be sketched directly onto the wood in preparation for sawing about the contour. The second point draws attention to the use of scraps. While not apparent in the finished object, two pieces make up the skier. The glue line remains hidden beneath the trunks. The assembly could only be made that way by having the grain run horizontally and in line with the character's extended arms, feet, and nose.

Surprise, especially when naively registered, makes a particularly good subject. A hunter given an expression of amazement is shown in Illus. 106, with the caption portraying his reception in the manner of a cartoon. Anyone who has ever brought a tough bird home to be cleaned should be able to identify with the situation.

The display is made of three species of wood,

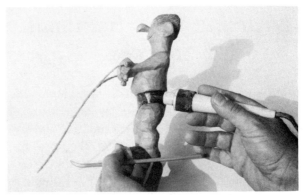

Illus. 105. Selective tinting and use of a burning tool add interest to the stylized character.

primarily due to availability. The hunter is basswood, the base pine, and the duck and gun aspen. Basswood and aspen respond quite well to the whittler's knife, but pine shows an interesting grain when varnished. Very likely the basswood figure would not create much interest if it had not been finished in color. Certainly, it would not be as realistic.

Illus. 106. This successful hunter seems to register complete surprise at the reception he receives.

Drawing from Inanimate Sources

Mathematics and science are sometimes drawn upon for the representation of botanical and geometric figures. Atomic, crystalline, and microscopic structures are among the less frequently used patterns for carving in the round. The problem with carving many of them is keeping the sections firm and substantial. For that reason, the parts are often carved with a supporting background.

An example of how solid the wood must be in certain applications may be sensed from the cutting board in Illus. 107. The carving, a pineapple motif, forms the grip of the board. The entire piece serves a practical function, with the conventionalized carving serving essentially a decorative purpose. A plain handle would function just about as well, but to develop a habit of leaving all such projects undecorated would ultimately result in an unattractive display of plain shapes.

In constructing a cutting board of this design, several points should be noted. The wood should be close-grained so that it can be easily kept clean, and both the board and the carving should be made without sharp corners in order to minimize wear. An occasional application of vegetable oil will help to protect the piece. Seasoned cherry wood, as used here, will meet the requirements adequately. Since a hole must be drilled where needed for hanging, the design should be made to accommodate it.

Designs of purely geometrical shape draw upon mathematics and, therefore, are unlike any previous examples in this chapter. Shapes from solid geometry are their basis. Cones, cylinders, spheres, and boxlike solids are fundamental ones, although many other mathematical constructs capable of being given body graphically fit the definition. Their use in carving produces a special type of design.

This type of woodcarving forms is the attraction of Illus. 108. The photograph shows how to position the knife when producing a helix (actually, a double helix) on a candlestick.

In order to construct the geometric pattern, two parallel spirals are first drawn equally spaced on a thoroughly dried stick. The grooves are hollowed along the lines by pressing a sharp blade against the round stock while rotating it in a firm and deliberate manner. With each turn of the piece, increasingly deeper cuts can be taken until, finally, the adjacent grooves come together. If the wood is not dried, the tackiness of the sap will make the process difficult. Finally the grooves are sanded by using a piece of abrasive wrapped about a finger.

Much of the beauty of the candlestick originates from the grain in the geometric pattern. Sumac, due to its variegated color, makes an ideal material for the purpose, and is why the geometric carving was finished in the natural.

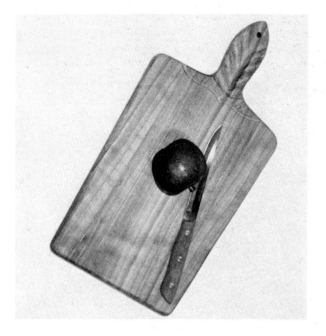

Illus. 107. The formalized motif carved on both sides of this cherry-wood cutting board makes an appropriate decoration.

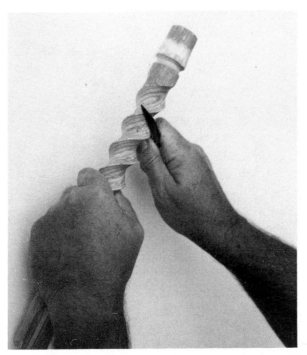

Illus. 108. Deeply carved geometric patterns in sumac should be finished in the natural to preserve the beautiful grain revealed.

Decorating with Overlays

Objects made by whittling or sculpturing are sometimes carved at less than full depth. The backs of figures are flat when intended for use in a wall decoration or for gluing to a surface. Designs for brooches are also carved that way. Generally, though, in these cases the art of composing mass, space, and form are the same as if for carving in the round.

Overlays are ordinarily glued to flat surfaces (boxes and cabinets), but some craftsmen undertake the additional step of inlaying a carving part way. This seems entirely unnecessary, since the appearance is nearly the same, and the strength of glues in use today makes it an extra and questionable effort.

Selection of the woods for contrast and purpose deserves full consideration, as in the project in Illus. 109. The flying geese were made from soft pine, the moon from cherry wood, and the coin box from black walnut. The pine and walnut could be reversed and comparable effect would

have resulted from gluing dark birds onto a light surface. The only minor use of inlaying is the head of the bird set into the moon, and its use is strictly practical.

As the designer dwells on the possibilities of overlays, many ideas will undoubtedly come to mind. Several woods in combination could be applied in an arrangement of flowers which, for example, uses cherry and walnut woods for the parts. Some light in color could also be carved and stained or tinted for effect. One-sided carvings of inanimate objects, including symbols and emblems, suggest even more potential ideas.

The placement of overlays on a backing of wood poses a problem not customarily encountered when designing free-standing sculptures. The solution lies in the method of handling background in relief-carving design.

Illus. 109. Carved overlays are like carvings in the round which have been halved lengthwise.

Using Color

The use of artificial color in carving evokes mixed emotions. While it is disdained by those who want nothing to show but the natural wood and evidence of the tooling, other persons hold a contrary view. They contend that color not only enhances the appearance of some carvings but that it should by all means be added to cover defects. Which point of view prevails in a given instance depends on both personal preferences and practical considerations (Illus. 110–111).

Although the use of color still seems to be a matter of individual choice, the philosophies prevailing in times past have noticeably impacted the practice. During the Middle Ages, carvings were considered to be more lifelike with their surfaces completely painted over. That practice diminished gradually, giving way largely to arguments for "truth of material." The arguments extended well into the twentieth century. While they continue to be espoused in some circles, an increase in the frequency of tinted and solidly colored carvings has come into view in recent years. Evidence of a new trend has now emerged.

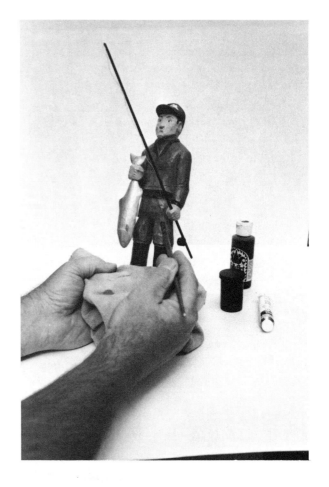

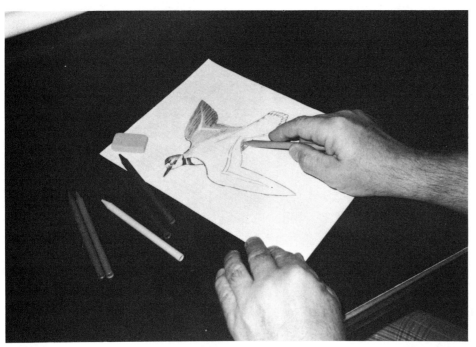

Illus. 110 (above). The tinting of a basswood whittling adds "character" and may be controlled by applying thin washes of acrylic paint after sealing the wood.

Illus. 111 (left). Adding color to a sketch can be a useful approach for some in preparation for painting a woodcarving.

The broader use of artificial color is apparent in carving of all kinds, and it seems likely to gain momentum in the future. Necessity is a major reason. Wood of the quality and sizes desired is becoming evermore scarce. As a result, opaque colors are gaining unequalled attention as an effective means of hiding unsightly fillers and glue lines in built-up sections of wood (Illus. 112–113).

Diminishing quality has become serious. Defective pieces that once would have been discarded out of hand now remain in use. Even some pieces tunnelled by wood borers are being kept for carving. (As a matter of fact, the editors of at least one publication advise woodcarvers on how to kill the borers in a microwave oven rather than discard the worm-infested wood. It works but it also indicates the seriousness of the carver's problem.)

In previous topics, the woodcarver was advised to take advantage of any opportunity to incorporate a knot in his design in place of having it appear as a blemish. The same was true for arranging the wood, to the extent possible, so that defects could be cut away with the waste. Those recommendations have not changed, and just now color has been proposed as another solution. By following those recommendations from the design stage through to the finish, a reasonably aware person should be able to transform his drawings into works of quality and artistic value.

Deciding whether or not to color a woodcarving represents only one aspect of a larger problem. An occasional woodcarver will build the problem to the proportions of a dilemma when deciding whether the process or the product holds more importance. The act and product of

Illus. 112. Opaque oil paints will completely cover blemishes and the disturbing appearance of glued-up sections of wood.

carving should be gratifying, and if not, a different medium of expression should be sought.

The crux of the problem is that the process-oriented craftsman may become so enraptured with his skill that he will want to show it above all else. Such could be his reason for bringing a project to an elaborate conclusion. Another person may argue that the artistic qualities of the creation—its design and the effectiveness of the interpretation—are primary, contending that the techniques and methods are secondary considerations, at best. While both approaches to the problem have merit, the craftsman must eventually come to the conclusion that lacking the quality of a good design, a carving has little if anything of significance about it.

Illus. 113. Painting is unequalled for imparting the preciseness of effect sometimes desired in animals.

VIII
DESIGN FOR UTILITY

An item designed for utility has a useful, rather than a decorative, purpose. It may function as a container, a tool, an instrument, or a machine. Emphasis centers on the specific use to which the product will be put, with the artistry involved being at least partly dependent on the form developed for the purpose.

Establishing Function

In product design, the disciplines of art and engineering tend to merge. Neither area of concern can fulfill requirements without affecting the other. Extremes must be avoided altogether; otherwise, the product will look good but function poorly, or the product will work well but lack beauty. An applicable expression in engineering holds: "If it doesn't look good, change it." This statement would seem to apply with equal force in the design of woodcarvings.

The importance of the relationship between form and function is seen in the boomerang in Illus. 114. Its shape and distributed mass determine how effective the device will be when given a twirling motion in flight. Every detail must be carved properly for it to operate without fault. The lines result not so much from attention to what will be beautiful as to the demands of throwing, spinning, and returning. Beauty results from the form so fashioned.

Some boomerangs are embellished with painted figures, but none of those adornments alters the basic shape or has a detrimental effect

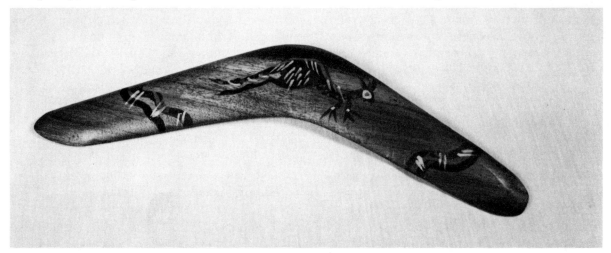

Illus. 114. The well-made boomerang is a classic example of form deriving from function, irrespective of any painting.

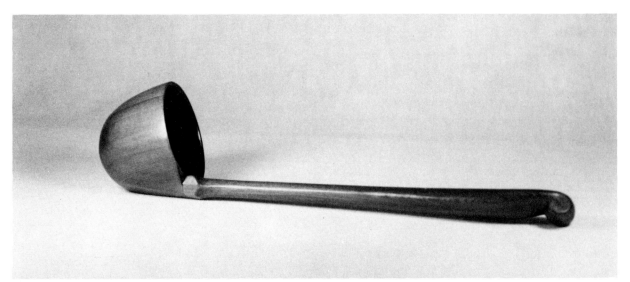

Illus. 115. A dipper made for use in a sauna also takes its basic form from meeting the requirements of the application.

on physical performance. A boomerang apparently works as well without paintings as with them, since the paintings have a nonutilitarian purpose.

A rule commonly accepted in the general practice of design is that *form follows function.* Thus, the primary determinant of shape must be use, insofar as economic considerations permit. Beauty of form cannot be ignored, but the designer who concentrates on it without regard to other factors may produce something entirely unacceptable.

Use may be the exclusive determinant of form for some craftsmen. For patternmakers and modelmakers, whose products almost always have practical application, that emphasis is necessary. Their work ordinarily serves an intermediate purpose. Unlike a woodcarver's products which remain in full view, their wooden creations do not have the visual appeal of those intended as end products.

When possible and permissible, a skilful designer will attempt to impart beauty to a practical object. He strives for harmony between appearance and function through an effective combination of mass and form. His primary concern is making products suitably useful but not unattractively mechanistic.

An appreciation for both appearance and use is

apparent in the design of the carving shown in Illus. 115. Having been planned for dipping water and splashing or sprinkling it onto hot stones in a sauna, the article has a handle of adequate length and a cup proportioned to the size needed. The assembly provides for gripping at a reasonable distance from the cup so the hand is safe from the energized heater. The length and position of the handle are also designed for dipping easily and deeply into a bucket of water.

Colorful, light-weight redwood was used in the two-piece construction. Although raw redwood withstands the effects of water better than most woods, a moisture-resistant clear finish was applied to help maintain the natural color. The end of the handle was dowelled for joining at the thick part of the cup, and waterproof glue secured the assembly. Since all surfaces were to be made smooth, a portion of the handle was widened before assembly to aid in gripping. The selection of wood for both parts constituted a major choice. Other rigid materials absorb and conduct heat, some becoming too hot to hold at the high temperatures of a sauna.

Several aspects of appearance were kept in mind when planning the dipper. A gracefully contoured cup was preferred, even though a straight-sided hollow cylinder would work about as well. The handle, too, could have been made cylindrical. A dowel rod would have made an easy solution. Instead, the parts were given a complementary contour so as to obtain a much more interesting design. While the parts joined in an aesthetic meshing of shapes, few features of the entire article were made strictly decorative. The terminal curls on the sides of the handle's tip, while adding little to usefulness, were a means of punctuating the dipper's lines in a visually harmonious way.

An important point to remember about designing utilitarian pieces is that a solution will not often be the sole answer. More than one solution will usually do. For that reason, a design must be evaluated primarily within itself and on the basis of objective criteria.

Designing Objectively

Objectivity has several meanings. In one sense, it means to design so that an object remains central to the carving. Reality may provide the inspiration. The result may or may not closely resemble an original form. In another sense, objectivity directs attention to an end result without subjective influence. Here, considerations of design prevail apart from the individual's feelings, assumptions, or other subjectively conceived ideas. This latter, nonsubjective approach becomes most essential in utilitarian design.

The better an article fulfills its purpose, the better its functional design. A design intended for practical application must first satisfy criteria pertaining to utility; then it must be made aesthetically pleasing. Consequently, a utilitarian design must meet two sets of criteria at the same time.

The utility of an object depends upon the design, construction, and material used. The combined impact can be considerable. A wooden dipper made from a single piece, for example, would likely be shaped similar to a scoop with the grain running lengthwise in the handle. Unless cut from a very thick section of wood, such a dipper will have to be designed for

holding in a cumbersome, horizontal position when dipping water. A two-piece design may be better.

The conditions necessary to carry out a useful purpose should be given careful thought in designing. A scoop for transferring finely ground flour at the kitchen counter illustrates the point. It must meet at least four conditions. First of all, it must hold a sufficient amount of the material. A design based on the cup measure will suffice when baking.

The second criterion is ease in filling. Gathering and removing the flour from its container must be considered at this stage. Flour is either kept in a special container or used directly from the sack as purchased. In either situation, a rigid shape easily pushed into the substance results in less spillage than one filled by pouring. A sharp leading edge is a good idea. Additionally, the article should be made long and rather narrow in order to reach to the bottom of the container.

Thirdly, the article must contain the flour somewhat compactly for ease in spotting it where needed, and the design must be able to withstand the force of tapping which frequently takes place alongside the edge of a baking utensil or mixing bowl. A lid on an article constructed to these requirements, for example, would seem to be more of an impediment than a benefit.

The material of construction makes the fourth, and last, major point to be considered. The wood should be easy to clean and handle. Therefore, it should be close-grained, lightweight, and smoothly finished.

The scoop in Illus. 116 fulfills the practical requirements outlined. The wood is aspen. The marks from tooling no longer show, and a durable, clear finish seals the sanded surface.

Clearly, the scoop will hold flour and similar substances, and the handle can be grasped normally either from above or around its ball-like end if scooping from a narrow sack. The tip of the handle, resting as it often will on a flat surface, also helps stabilize the scoop in an upright position. The fact that the handle has not been totally rounded helps in gripping and preventing slipping.

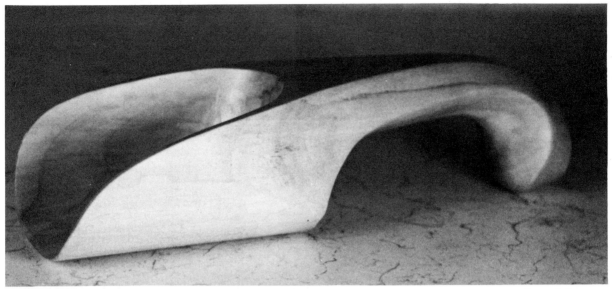

Illus. 116. The design of woodcarvings having more than one possible solution focuses on utility while giving attention to eye-appealing qualities.

In addition to suitability of size and shape, the scoop imparts a sense of visual comfort and correctness of balance, proportion, and mass. It contains no intricate or ornate details to detract from its use, while presenting more than the plain shape of an ordinary scoop. The artisan's awareness of material, design, and construction has resulted in a new arrangement of a piece which retains the practicality of earlier designs.

Applying Methodology

Designing for utility should be systematic. The idea is to give order to all necessary factors so that none are overlooked. The factors to consider are use, material, construction, and artistic appeal.

As a matter of general procedure, the objective determination of use most readily proceeds by posing questions about function. For instance, if the article is to hold something, what shall it hold and how much? Should it be made deep or wide? Should it be given a cover, and how will it be gripped normally? The designer must answer these questions at the outset. Other points of a similar nature may have to be considered, depending on the use intended for the article.

Selecting material poses a different set of considerations. Will the piece's use require wood which is soft or hard, light or dark, open- or close-grained, and air- or kiln-dried? When several species satisfy the demands, the selection then occurs according to ease of carving, beauty, and availability.

As to method of construction, the only requirement is to develop the object's form. Any machine or tool that enables a skillful craftsman to achieve his goal will do. A band saw and a scroll saw, on occasion, are useful for roughing out pieces before carving. The carving method remains the craftsman's choice. The pieces illustrated in Illus. 117 and Illus. 118 could be carved by hand or with power tools as long as the surfaces are sanded smooth.

Beauty should not be the least of the considerations in utilitarian design and, certainly, not the last. Attention should be directed to it along with the emergence of form for a practical use. Art work that looks like an ornamental afterthought can be very disconcerting. The only thing more disturbing is the kind of adornment which gets in the way of the product's performance. All such impediments and shortcomings should be eliminated at the design stage.

In most instances, carved decorations can be

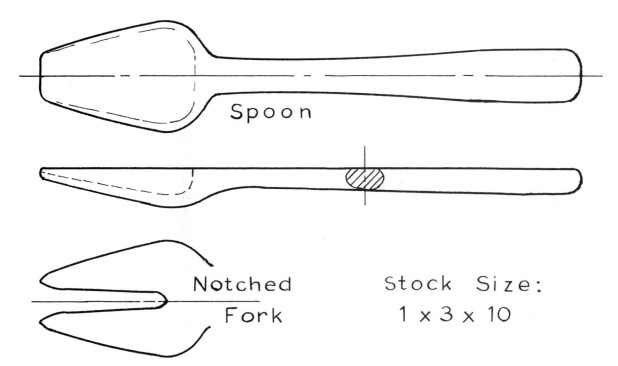

Spoon

Notched
Fork

Stock Size:
1 x 3 x 10

Illus. 117. A carved salad set is both useful and decorous.

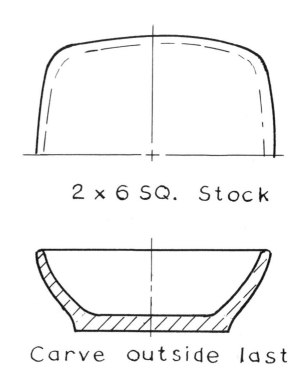

2 x 6 SQ. Stock

Carve outside last

Illus. 118. Individual salad bowls of wood also remain popular.

added without creating any discernible detraction, either visually or functionally. The achievement of good design depends on placing the decorations where they will serve as enhancements without impairing use.

Decorating Utilitarian Articles

Some functional pieces may be decorated more extensively than others, and some should not be decorated at all. The scoop in Illus. 116 represents those which need no decorating. Both the unique shape and the useful purpose of the piece are the reasons. On the other hand, the walking stick in Illus. 119 and Illus. 120 provides an opposite example.

The example shows how decoration and utility have been combined in a single piece. A walking stick functions primarily as a hiker's protective piece, defending against possible attack and the slashing of twigs in wooded areas. It will usually be grasped around its circumference near the thicker end and be moved along with each step much in the manner of a cane. A strong, lightweight, reasonably straight branch of ground-to-elbow length satisfies design purposes. To protect the stick from wearing too rapidly, a large oval- or round-headed wood screw may be driven into the ground end. The normal grip of the hand, the observer should note, does not exactly form a line at right angle with the fore-

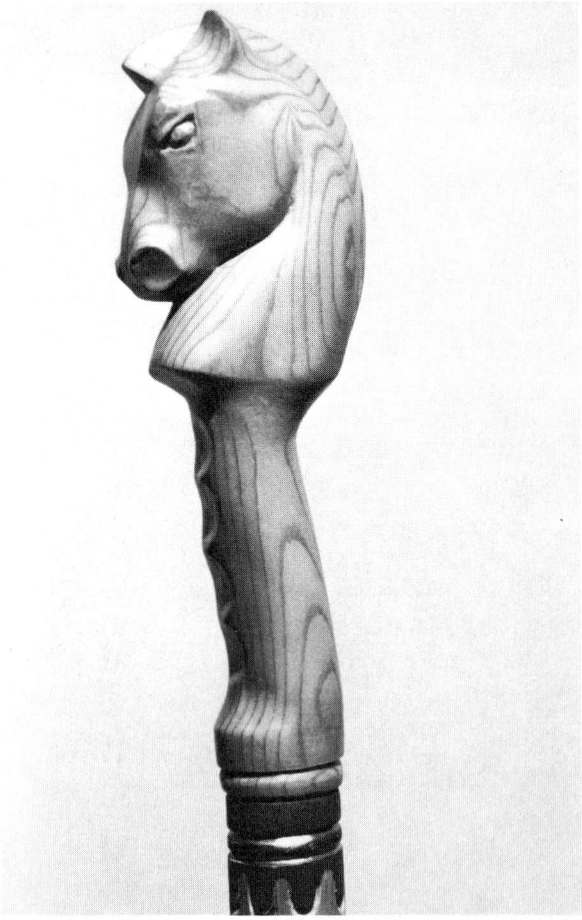

Illus. 119. The carving on this walking stick has a functionally designed handgrip with decorative parts above and below.

Illus. 120. The horse (carved from spruce) has been intentionally stylized to appear aggressive.

arm. The prolonged, firm gripping of such a stick therefore requires a handle that is quite unlike that on a flour scoop. Comfort becomes much more critical.

While a plain stick could be made to fulfill all the requirements of utility, a decorative element or two adds individuality to a device of commonplace form. Plainness and sameness, of course, are the conditions under which decoration should be applied. The embellishment may have a serious, unemotional, or humorous side. The stick in Illus. 119 and Illus. 120 has a horse's head carved in an aggressive mood. The wood in this stylized version, along with the hand grip, is from a spruce 2 x 4. The piece is securely fixed with tenon and glue at the end of an aspen shaft from which the bark had been removed. Shallow carving and bright colors adorn the juncture of the pieces. The design about that point symbolizes the colorful harness once used on show horses. Nothing more need be added.

The cane in Illus. 121 affords a comparison. An important difference between the walking stick and this cane comes about because of a change in use. A cane should be made to reach the thigh so as to be leaned on. Thus, the hand must hold the cane around its top end.

Nothing sharp or rough should impede holding. The smooth ball makes an adequate support for moderate forces. It can be easily held, and it distributes pressure in the palm. The rhythmic spiral in the geometric decoration goes well with the spherical shape at the cane's head. Again a bit of paint creates a lively contrast.

Instead of artificial color, a little extra carving sometimes can do the job. The serving tray in Illus. 122 has spotted on it two simple but interesting carvings. They are done in two-plane relief, with a stippled background. Their presence in no way alters the purpose of holding nuts or candies, nor does their use impair lifting and carrying by hand. The decorations effectively offset the plainness of the formalized shape and the smoothness of the finished cherry wood.

Two points should be observed when constructing a tray of this kind. First, the carving of the central cavities should be done before the

Illus. 121. The sphere on this cane makes an appropriate grip for supporting moderate weight and effectively complements the other geometric shapes.

Illus. 122. The appearance of a carved tray of plain form can be improved when planned for decorating with shallow relief carvings.

more delicate decorations. The other point has to do with lifting and holding. The base should be made part of the design so that the edge of the tray will be slightly elevated. A ⅝-inch elevation will do.

Designing Wooden Ware

Not many years ago, wooden kitchen utensils of considerable quantity were a common thing. Their use has diminished with time to the point where only a few such items are available commercially. Salad bowls, serving forks, stirring spoons, and hollowed trays in assorted shapes and sizes are among the items that have remained. For the most part, modern methods have now replaced the earlier practice of hand-carving the wooden ware.

Hand-carved trays are still very popular. One reason is the beauty of the material. Another relates to the preference for handling things made of wood. Then, too, beautifully shaped trays are likely to receive the attention of others without the housewife calling attention to them. Their use as centerpieces when not being handled in serving attests to the desirability of the pieces.

The design of wooden ware, as in design generally, should be orderly. The advantages of following a set procedure may be entirely clear, but the simultaneous occurrence of some steps in an order of progression should also be recognized. The most important concern is that adequate attention be given to the major points in the process.

First, determine the proposed use, or uses, for the article. If several uses are intended they must be compatible, or the article will not be adequate in all instances. A tray could be properly designed to hold either candy mints or sugar cubes, but a single design would not be entirely effective when intended for holding mints at one time and apples at another.

Is the article for holding, pouring, or spreading? The information is extremely important, for each purpose brings with it a different form. A shape may be only vaguely conceived at this stage.

After determining what the carving is to do, the designer must decide how to do it. This phase of design necessitates the gathering of facts.

Size of the object becomes an essential consideration. If it will be used in serving, knowing the amount of the substance or the quantity of the items normally served will help in making a determination of dimensions. The designer must also know how the article will be moved from one place to another. An item for serving is a device for transferring things by hand. Perhaps, handles will be needed. Additionally, the item must be shaped to resist tipping and spilling. Think about the difference between a tray for holding cups or glasses and one for serving shelled peanuts.

Along with the list of facts related to use, the designer must concentrate on matters of material

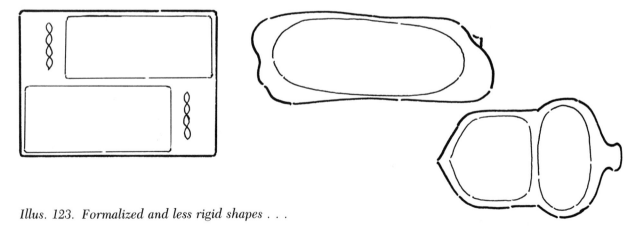

Illus. 123. Formalized and less rigid shapes . . .

and construction. Available woods of the best color, grain, and density should be chosen. The suitability of the wood for carving to the form intended poses another consideration, and wood that will not easily chip when carved thinly should be selected for articles such as serving trays. Whether the design calls for a smoothly contoured or intricately detailed surface makes a substantial difference, as well.

The next step in the process tests the designer's ability to develop the idea graphically. He begins by making trial sketches. The proportions must be kept in balance while varying the shapes. Mass, unity, repetition, and style are other matters to keep in mind.

Since mass and form are the primary factors in utilitarian design, the designer should give them his utmost attention. If planning a serving tray, quick sketches of the outlines are a good way to make a number of trials from which to choose. A section or two showing the carved thickness of the wood completes the drawing.

After thoroughly defining purpose, collecting facts, and applying an artist's touch in drawing, the designer should select the best of his designs. The choice should be pleasing and workable. If several designs seem to fill the bill, as could be the case in Illus. 123, he should make the selection according to the preference of the person who will use the article. An individual's inclination for things taken from nature or for those contrived in some other way ordinarily shows in the decorations in the home. The design chosen serves as the basis for further development.

The final step in preparing for the actual carving pertains to the analysis of the design selected. All aspects of the plan must be scrutinized. The opinion of a second party could be helpful, because a single weakness unseen by the designer may be the first thing noticed by an independent observer. Following the review, the designer has the option of proceeding with the plan as it is, bringing it to a higher level of refinement, or of rejecting it totally and starting over. As often as not, the conscientious designer changes his first design or develops another. The situation most vexing of all is to have a design made into a finished product and then to realize it simply fails to measure up to expectations. The advice of a knowledgeable, independent observer can be a means of avoiding disappointment later.

A craftsman may occasionally find reason to alter a design as he enters into the carving of a piece, whether it be because of uncovering of a resin duct or other defect, or his realization of the need to make the carving easier by slightly changing a shape. He also may lack equipment for making deep cuts, such as the bent gouge shown in Illus. 124. Changes of those kinds should always be made with care, for they are likely to have mixed results.

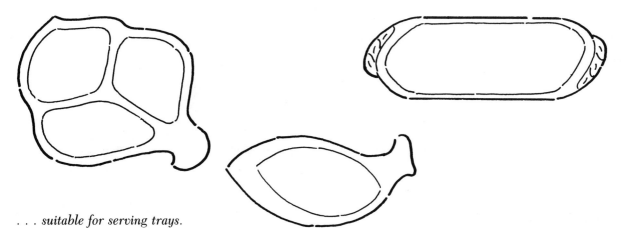

. . . suitable for serving trays.

101

Illus. 124. An adjustable bench stop, mallet, and gouges are useful in bringing a hardwood tray to the shape intended.

Selecting a Finish

The type of finish selected for a wooden article depends, basically, on its intended use. An object designed for serving food should most certainly be coated with a nontoxic substance. Vegetable oil rubbed into the surface is good. Salad bowls, stirring spoons, and dishes for holding wet or somewhat acidic foods may be so treated. Of course, oils that have a strong flavor should be avoided. Mineral oil may be a good alternative.

The use of oil has an inherent disadvantage in that periodic applications are necessary. Recently developed products specially designed for coating wooden food containers avoid that problem. Either way, the protection and beautification afforded makes the application worthwhile.

Staining is not recommended for wooden ware. Appearance is part of the reason. A clear, hard finish might temporarily seal in the stain, but carved ware exhibit a large amount of end grain. That condition virtually eliminates uniformity of color by staining. Due to the more serious possibilities from the stain seeping out, carved kitchen utensils and trays are almost always finished in the natural. The wood should be selected accordingly. The mahogany from which the small trays in Illus. 125 were carved presents a colorful grain when coated with a cooking oil.

For other kinds of utilitarian products, the polyurethanes on the market are quite acceptable. They are easily brushed on, produce a mar-resistant surface, and many of them are unaffected by water. The moisture-resistant ones are easy to clean. Polyurethanes also give the craftsman a choice about glossiness. A dull or satin sheen can be obtained without the labor of hand-rubbing. When carefully applied, these clear finishes bring out the grain in a manner difficult to surpass. Thin coats are best, since heavily applied layers result in undesirable build-up.

The utility of a carving depends on practically everything from the initial design to the final finish. This is also true of a carving's artistic appeal. As with artistry and utility, so with form and function. The inter-relationships cannot be ignored at any stage of development or construction.

Illus. 125. A nontoxic oil used in cooking makes a good finish on products for containing olives or other edibles.

IX
CARVED WOODTURNING DESIGN

Woodcarving designs must be made to suit the shapes of the surfaces being decorated. Up to now, the surfaces have been basically flat. When working with woodturnings, the focus is on techniques for decorating areas having a roundness of form. The carvings are applied to curvilinear surfaces almost exclusively, except for the flat ends of cylindrical pieces.

All shapes produced by ordinary methods of woodturning derive from the cylinder and sphere, despite any intricate surface configuration in a design. Even though a piece may be irregularly contoured, close analysis reveals a basic cylindrical or spherical curvature of the parts. The rotary motion of wood against tool produces the shapes.

Decorating Circular Areas

Circular patterns make excellent designs for woodturnings, whether placed on flat tops or spherically curved lids of boxes.

An area bounded by a circular edge may be carved in any of several basic forms. It may be embellished with a borderlike band, be given a centrally confined location, or be decorated all-over. The decoration's outer extremities should fall within and generally be equidistant to the circular edge.

Although narrow bands are sometimes carved around a circumference, boxes of cylindrical shape are usually decorated on top. Both incised and relief carving are suitable, and they can be tooled about as easily on woodturnings as on other products.

A series of overlapping circles makes an interesting design when chip carved. The circles complement an area's boundary, and they can be varied in size, number, and pattern. They are drawn directly on the wood with a compass after first accurately locating the center. Illus. 126 shows a finished application. Much of its attractiveness is due to the depth of the carving.

A bench hook aids considerably when carving small circular patterns, especially if one side has been notched. A round piece can be held and rotated in the V without clamping.

Woodturnings intended for chip carving should, if convenient, be left a little thicker where the design will be placed. The increased thickness will provide for deep tooling, as chip carvings produce strong shadow lines if boldly carved. The carvings not only show greater contrast that way, but deep incising offsets the slightly increased weight from the additional wood. That consideration may be most important in the design of a lightweight box.

Illus. 126. Deeply cut chip carvings make impressive decorations on woodturnings.

Decorating Other Shapes

Woodturnings are sometimes decorated with ribbonlike carvings aligned circumferentially. Those designs, much like border patterns, have repetitiously arranged details. Their alternating or sequentially rhythmic patterns make them a highly pleasing decoration. Additionally, the cylinder's curvature creates interest by the fore-shortening of details along the receding surface.

When decorating a project, a series of intervals can be pencilled on a piece of paper long enough to go around the cylinder at the point to be decorated. The total distance around the piece can then be divided into intervals by transferring the marked distances with the paper strip wrapped about. This simplifies the work and eliminates the need to measure the diameter and calculate the circumference. It also replaces trial-and-error stepping with dividers. The complete process, from preparation to finishing, is shown in Illus. 127–135. This knowledge can be invaluable for the designer.

On large cylinders, the dividers may prove to be more convenient than the paper strip. The circumference can be calculated by multiplying the piece's diameter by 3.14. The distance must then be divided into equal intervals for marking the piece all around.

Of equal consequence is the determination of spacing of the intervals to be marked off. A matter of artistic presentation applies here. The interval should provide for full viewing of a repeated segment. In other words, the viewer must be able to take in an entire unit of the design at once without having to turn it or study it from a second position. The requirements of proportion must be satisfied, as well.

An article such as the one in Illus. 136 should always be designed for a specific purpose. This

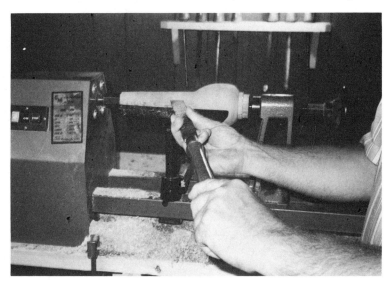

Illus. 127. The decorative process proceeds from proper shaping . . .

Illus. 128. Thorough sanding before adding the layout . . .

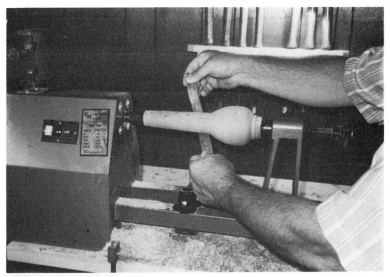

Illus. 129. Pencilling in the design's location . . .

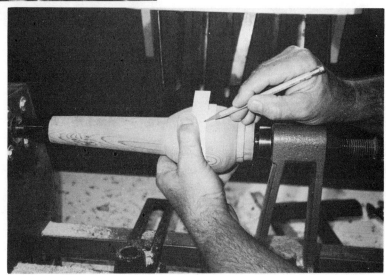

Illus. 130. Marking the circumference on a paper strip . . .

Illus. 131. Dividing the circumference equally . . .

Illus. 132. Transferring the marks to the woodturning . . .

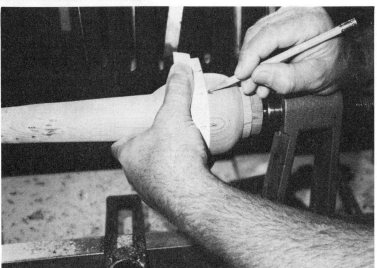

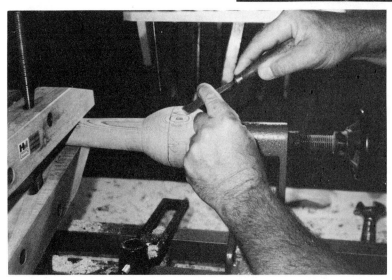

Illus. 133. Carving the design in the lathe . . .

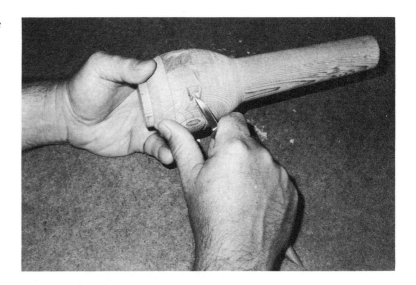

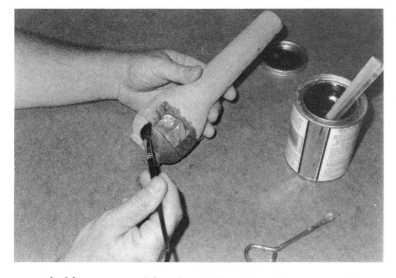

Illus. 135. Applying a clear protective finish after hollowing the stem by drilling.

piece holds cuttings of dried cattails and reeds. A 1-inch hole about 6 inches deep in the vase's stem holds the arrangement of plants. The enlarged mass near the base stabilizes the object and, at the same time, better accommodates a decorative carving.

While the design's features are essentially abstract, their leaf-like pattern appears to be fully compatible with the article's use. Its dimensions and placement are equally effective. A finish of satin polyurethane makes the decorated vase stand out in harmony with the arrangement.

Motif, size, and placement are among the variables to take into account in circumferential design. Because of the special nature of the applications, several unique visual requirements must be observed. One pertains to vertical positioning. Designs placed on vertical articles should have an upright orientation so that, if done in realistic style, they will not appear to be radical violations of nature.

Another point pertains to measurements and distance. The width of a carved band should not be the same as the distance from the band to the edge. Neither should the band seem to be too close to an end. The designer must keep in mind that objects viewed from above or below will be visually foreshortened. To counteract that effect, a measurement may have to be increased somewhat. A corollary occurs in the design of statuary.

Illus. 136 (left). The finished redwood vase, with its finely styled and well-proportioned carving, makes an excellent accessory for cuttings of cattails.

Illus. 137 (above). Designs for incising in continuous repetition make good circumferential decorations on woodturnings.

A statue made for placing much above street level must have its torso unnaturally lengthened so as to appear normal from below. The amount of such foreshortening depends on scale and distance.

Although foreshortening could present a problem in some instances, normal woodturning carving presents a different sort of concern. Questions of need and type come forth. A decoration should be used only if the piece would be too plain or uninteresting without it. Given this need, an equally difficult decision must be made about the form of the design—whether in several spots, arranged vertically or horizontally, or made continuously circumferential. Some possible suggestions are given in Illus. 137.

The designer of woodturnings must be aware that the user will handle and move the finished piece. That habit has significance for the placement of a carving, especially a circumferential one. At times the view will be from above and at others more directly to the side. Thus, the article should have the decoration positioned as in Illus. 138. The carving optically-placed appears far preferable to the one placed in the middle. Foreshortening will not adversely affect this decoration. The areas above and below the carving will appear to maintain the same relative proportions from all angles.

As in woodcarving generally, the craftsman who decorates woodturnings should take careful account of the amount of adornment for his

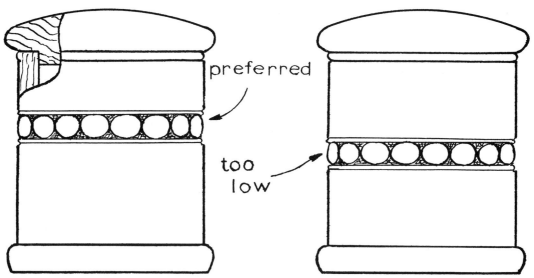

Illus. 138. The location of a carved decoration can affect an article's appearance either favorably or unfavorably.

projects. The best practices avoid an overelaborate mixing and amassing of artistic details. An inharmonious grouping of extravagantly carved ornamentation is called *rococo*. The term derives from the style that had its heyday in the seventeenth and eighteenth centuries. Today, it is considered excessive and in bad taste. The advice offered the craftsman is to concentrate on keeping his decorations uncluttered. When uncertain about the result (something that plagues us all at times), it is preferable to err on the side of simplicity than endure the cost of overembellishment.

Eliminating Background Detail

There are practical, as well as aesthetic, reasons for keeping decorations simple. Woodturnings present special carving problems. Designs which avoid fragile detailing and extra care in handling are preferred. A practical solution is to use

Illus. 139. Inextravagant carving is far preferable to the overelaborate amassing of detail called rococo.

subjects that require little or no background tooling. That is why designs for incising sometimes work best.

The walnut pencil holder in Illus. 139 contains an example of the kind of carving suggested. Uncomplicated styling characterizes the design. Since the figures are recessed, the article can be handled without being easily damaged.

For those who prefer relief carving, the article must be clamped during construction so that no damaging pressure will be placed on the carved details. Usually, an object to be carved around its perimeter will have to be secured along the line of the axis of rotation. A vise may work for a small object, but a large one will probably require use of a jig or special positioning while mounted in the lathe.

The relief carving of woodturnings must meet the demands of the design. A decorative perimeter on a bowl must be specially treated. To begin with, the wood should be shaped and smoothed around the outside only so that the edge carving can be done before turning the

Illus. 140, a determination of the carving's greatest width and depth must be made before turning the part. In that way a ridge can be provided from which the forms will be created. The carving will remove wood from around the design to the level of the larger turned surface so that the carved forms seem to project outward.

Vines with leaves are only one of many possibilities. Continuous geometric figures also make interesting patterns around the perimeter of boxes and bowls. A regularity of pattern and uniformity of sequence are always expected in such decorations.

Whittling Turned Pieces

Carving woodturnings has the same general purpose as carving objects from blocks or flat pieces. Although the design considerations present slightly different concerns, the uses remain very much the same. The whittling of woodturnings,

Illus. 140. The design on this pine bowl has been left raised in bold relief about the perimeter.

center. An easy clamping arrangement can then be devised by positioning the flats at the piece's center between the jaws of a large wooden handscrew. The heel of the handscrew, in turn, can be clamped in a vise or to the bench top while doing the carving.

Since the design will be raised as shown in

as with incising and relief carving, is done mainly for decoration.

Preparing a woodturning for whittling has much the same purpose as removing excess wood by bandsawing around an outline prior to carving. The difference is that no more than a single profile can be traced in the lathe.

Illus. 141. Hardwood chess pieces in contemporaneous design can be turned on the lathe so that only the knight requires much carving.

The chess pieces in Illus. 141 were made by turning and whittling. Only one required much carving. The design followed the practice of permitting substantial leeway as long as continuity of form remains evident. Although generally not necessary, a dense hardwood was used to obtain a sharpness of detail and durability under use.

Since woodturning produces pieces having cylindrical or spherical curvatures, whittling serves only to modify those shapes in some way. A slender, cylindrical candlestick could be given a whittled decoration of concave or convex spirals, and a small knob on the top of a turned box lid could be shaped with a knife into one of any number of figures. The handles of letter openers could also be made that way. The main concern is to avoid using details which impede gripping.

Incising with Power Tools

The general practice of woodworking with power tools seems to affect people in different ways. Craftsmen now widely accept the use of ma-

chines in the making of furniture, and not many people prefer to make woodturnings on a hand-powered lathe anymore. Carving with electrically powered tools, on the other hand, evokes a more mixed reaction. A point held against power carving is the telltale rounding sometimes left in grooved work. Interestingly, proponents of the exclusive use of hand-carving expound on the merits of leaving marks. The contention seems to hold with some that the identifiable characteristics of tooling by hand are preferable to those resulting from electrically driven tools. The logic follows that things obviously hand-carved are each different, while machine-made articles of a given design all look alike. The distinction is notable.

When individually controlled power tools are used, the details will occasionally stand as carved (Illus. 143). Some craftsmen make no attempt to alter appearance in any manner. A design incised with a power tool and left to stand unaltered decorates the fruit bowl in Illus. 144. Only the leaves are the result of hand-carving.

The roundness of the incisions on the fruit bowl offers little doubt as to which cuts were

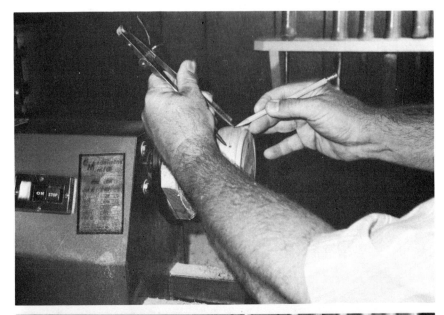

Illus. 142. Designs about a circumference are sometimes most easily marked off with dividers.

Illus. 143. Incising with a high-speed power tool often works best with the project in the lathe.

Illus. 144. Evidence of carving done with a power tool shows in the rounded cuts on this bowl.

made with a high-speed cutting burr. The carver who has no difficulty accepting such features may find the work can be readily done with the piece mounted in the lathe, while remaining aware that greater design flexibility comes with incising with hand tools.

While hand-carving and incising with power tools are quite different, the principles of design governing the two remain essentially the same, especially those appropos to decoration. Above all, a carving should not be applied to a woodturning that has no suitable place for it. As with the fruit bowl, the design must be placed on the outside of a project and in an easily viewed spot.

Embellishing Functional Pieces

There are times when the rounded shapes of woodturnings are just too plain. That condition has become more and more prevalent over the years as the trend towards streamlined design has taken hold. Streamlining can be effective, but one smooth shape after another can be too much. A carefully applied design may make the difference. Many pieces as carved make attractive decorations, apart from any other intended use. Ideas along this line are seen in the several sketches of woodturnings in Illus. 145.

An effective means of decorating a woodturning is gouging. Closely spaced, irregular cuts are preferred. A random pattern created in that manner can be seen on the candlestick in Illus. 146.

Here, again, design was closely related to construction. The texture was applied after shaping the body of each candle holder in the lathe. With the lathe centers gripping the ends—one to be drilled for the metal insert and the other shaped for fitting into the base—the body piece remained sufficiently fixed for the hand-carving. A balance of visual interests was achieved by giving the end portions a smooth finish.

An adornment should never impede or in any manner have a negative effect on the purpose for which the object has been made. Most woodturnings are made for a practical reason, so the decoration must create visual interest without interfering with that use. A pierced design cut into a dish for holding small mints might be attractive, but the opportunities for the candies to lodge in or fall through the pierced openings

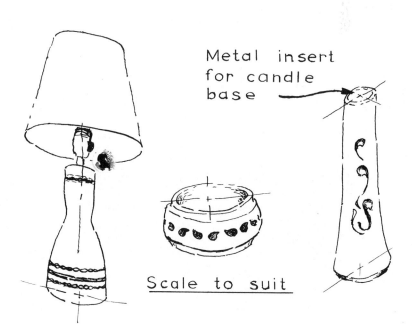

Illus. 145. Some plain woodturnings can be decorated to advantage with shallow carvings.

Metal insert for candle base

Scale to suit

Illus. 146 (left). Surfaces roughened by gouging, although very ornamental, tend to hide blemishes uncovered by turning.

Illus. 147 (below). This carefully decorated spice shaker serves beautifully when grilling outdoors.

could have detrimental consequences. Obviously, a design of another form would be better in this instance.

Another design consideration relates to form and use. A carving with very delicate projections would be entirely inappropriate on an object that will be firmly handled. This point bears observing if for no other reason than the reluctance of an intended user to grasp the piece for fear of causing damage. An incised carving may afford a better solution, as with the spice shaker in Illus. 147. The finely carved figures have absolutely no purpose aside from their aesthetic effect.

A spice shaker used outdoors when grilling will likely be subjected to extensive handling, and not always in a delicate manner. There need be no fear of this carving either breaking or wearing away. Even regular use about a heated grill will not do damage. The firmness of the cherry wood contributes to durability, and a finish which has qualities of durability and resistance to the elements further protects the piece.

What kinds of designs are appropriate for the article? Many. Two stylized bands, an over-all geometric pattern, or a small realistic scene on the front are immediate examples.

Important to the application is the use of shallow carving, either incised or relieved. The point of attachment of the handle may influence the placement of the decoration by whatever means carved. It, in fact, is the reason the vertical design shown was placed in three locations instead of four.

The turning of wood with hand-held tools, as with the beautification of products by hand-carving, has practically disappeared as a trade. Most of such work now falls within the province of hobbyists and an occasional professional craftsman. Automatic woodturning machines produce articles much more in keeping with the demands of commercial production. Pottery is also used in the production of kitchen wares once made of wood. Because of these developments and others like them, individually constructed products are generally far more limited in sphere of distribution.

Credit for attempting to perpetuate the art of selective design goes to the craftsman who continually engages in handcrafting. The charm of woodturnings skillfully adorned with individualized carvings, no matter how small, stands apart in sharp contrast to the many run-of-the-mill products widely distributed in the marketplace. A conscientious designer may experience the joy of being able to create something which has artistic appeal, while knowing it to be the only one of its kind. That incentive can be truly compelling.

X
BORDER AND EDGE DECORATION

Carving along the perimeter of a surface has basis in art. The reasons for decorating that way are: to terminate or frame a design; to draw attention to grain within an outline; to balance an off-center design; to fill a void between a design and edge; and simply to add decoration. One or more of these reasons must be present or there will be no need for the carving.

Decorations at or near an edge may be formed by the methods of relief carving and incising, or by their use in combination. Some of the designs are similar to the scalloped decorations carpenters saw along the sides of valance boards. The carving of edgings affords far greater flexibility.

Designing Borders

A border design must relate to the central point of emphasis and to the overall shape of the piece. This requirement means giving the border a configuration much the same as the perimeter. The carving forms an outline slightly removed from the edge, with its detail contrived so as to complement the work within.

The designer must exercise good judgment when forming a border. He must realize, initially, that some woodcarvings do not require outlining. The edge of a decoration alone may function appropriately. In some cases, a border will give a crowded appearance that would be seriously detrimental.

The detail making up a border should be kept to a minimum. The plan must show restraint and concern for the totality of the arrangement, as an elaborate or highly intricate border will often detract from other features. An analogy which vividly exemplifies the need is seen in the lavishly carved picture frames that were so common around the turn of the century. The amount of ornamentation used violates a rule now widely accepted: A border should not be a conspicuous detraction no matter how beautiful it appears to be by itself. Fortunately, the elaborately carved frames of the past and the moulded plaster imitations which followed are no longer in general use.

Rules which precisely guide the designing of borders do not exist. Judgment has the major part. Whether or not to use a border, how much detail to provide, how much clearance to allow, and what method of carving to use will all depend on the situation. There are no hard and fast guidelines. However, the usual practices still hold. Decisions about space, balance, centering, symmetry, etc., must be made as before. Compatibility is an exceptional concern.

Parts of a design must be in harmony, one with another. Styles should not conflict. A geometrically carved border of triangles or zigzags would be completely incompatible with most naturalistic designs, while a groove or bead in a straight line will go with almost any pattern. The neutral shapes make a difference.

The bead formed by the groove along the edge of the plaque in Illus. 148 shows how effective an unobtrusively shaped border can be. It does not repeat any part of the center carving, but it does tie the design together simply by bounding the area of interest in the shape of the outline. Most importantly, it appears to be part of the construction.

Upon viewing the plaque, knowledgeable woodworkers will immediately realize that not just the central design was made by hand-carving. The shapes at points of intersection along the perimeter reveal that fact. Woodcarvers are advised to apply this form to grooving and beading along the edges of their creations. A more complicated carving is not needed in many instances.

The intended use and location of the piece also matters. A carving intended for use in a small child's room, such as on a border around a chalk board, could be made wider and more fantastic than most. A string of comical animals marching about in a line may create the desired interest. Designs for teenagers should reflect a bit more maturity. A series of flowers could do for a girl's room, while the mechanical look of a geometric carving may be better for a boy's. In such circumstances, both the style and motif of the design are dependent upon where the finished work will be normally placed and viewed.

Applications of different styles, motifs, and methods of carving will be found among the border designs in Illus. 149. Nature and geometry are the sources here, with several designs leaning toward the abstract. Their diversity indicates the leeway possible when creating borders.

Carving techniques add further flexibility to border decorating. Incising may be done in broad or narrow cuts, and relief carvings may be made shallow or deep. For most purposes, the less bold cuts give the desired result.

Illus. 150 shows an unusual arrangement. A partial border offsets the bold relief carving in the thick piece of buckeye wood. The design of this wall decoration indicates why border and subject should "agree." The border, as all borders should be, is made part of the design and not an unrelated addition. Without it, the relief carving could not be placed to a side. The straight lines hold the composition in balance and much in concert with the outer edges of the carving. The application shows how powerful a few slender lines can be.

For a more complete description of the possibilities, review the drawings of geometric outlines given in Chapters 5 and 6. The designs make suitable borders for certain applications. The drawings show, also, several alternate forms of corner detailing.

Illus. 148. The groove and bead carved along the edge of this piece satisfies design purposes without detracting from the central subject.

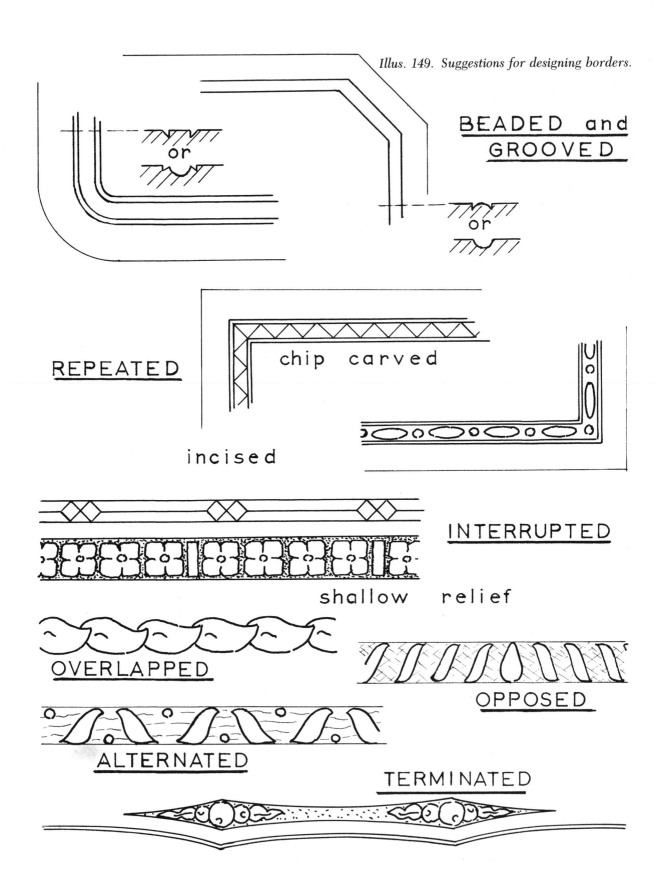

Illus. 149. Suggestions for designing borders.

BEADED and GROOVED

or

or

REPEATED

chip carved

incised

INTERRUPTED

shallow relief

OVERLAPPED

OPPOSED

ALTERNATED

TERMINATED

Repeating Details

Illus. 150. A bold relief carving (in buckeye) counterbalanced by a partial border makes a striking display on a den wall of brick.

Repetition is useful. Shapes placed end to end or side by side in a pattern create a highly unified appearance. The design instills in the viewer a sense of unbroken continuity, particularly when the elements are pointed in a line. Because of its agreeable impact, the repetition of detail is common practice in border design.

A string of repeated elements can also produce an effect close to disinterest. It results from the sameness of shapes. The observer need not, and usually will not, study each detail along an entire strip. The eye seems to notice the similarity and accept it without making an effort to scrutinize each section. When the line of sight wanders from the central subject, the repetitively detailed border only momentarily holds one's interest. A well-designed border of small details usually contains the view in this manner.

Borders of large details present a somewhat different picture. Those designed to stand alone in an effort to gain attention illustrate the point. Parades of animals on an article for a young person, as in Illus. 151, are indicative of a reason for making a border rather conspicuous.

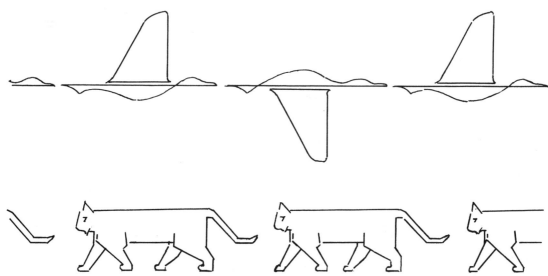

Illus. 151. Strings of animals, simplified and repeated, are also suitable as borders on some articles.

Illus. 152. A drawing board and instruments are most useful when developing geometric designs.

Nearly all borders incorporate repetition. Even a uniform groove will reveal identical cross-sections along its length. When failure occurs, something besides the sameness of repeated detail is probably to blame. Most likely, it is an inappropriate size, placement, or shape of a detail or details. The need for careful planning seems obvious.

A full unit should be drawn on paper when planning a border, and it should be repeated a sufficient number of times to enable the designer to judge its adequacy. Drawing instruments (Illus. 152) are indispensable when constructing strips of geometric elements repeated. The designer should also keep in mind that a shape repeated in a line will likely be overbearing to the adult viewer when made very large. Drawing helps identify such conditions. If the design seems as if it will attract attention unduly, it should be changed before carving. A comparison of designs may be needed beforehand.

Using Corner Fillers

A special technique in the artistry of carving is filling corner spaces on rectangular surfaces. The decorations are customarily restricted so that the grain of the wood or an applied design remains in view in the center. The outer designs may be connected by a continuous border for a unifying

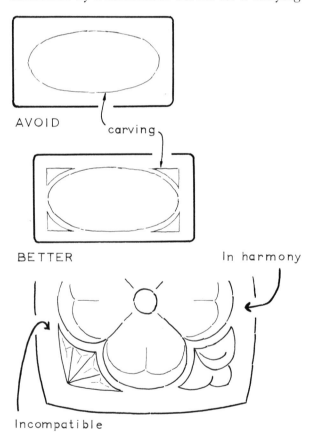

Illus. 153. Adapting carvings to fixed shapes with corner fillers.

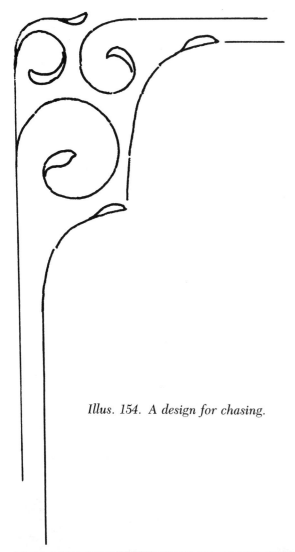

Illus. 154. A design for chasing.

Illus. 155. This small candy dish shows how a carving can be incorporated to advantage in a balanced design.

effect, or they may be left alone when warranted. The corners become a point of interest and variety in either instance. Some thoughtfully and cleverly designed fillers will direct the viewer's sight back to the middle (Illus. 153).

When decorating vertically-mounted panels, corner fillers should be treated as a single unit. Optical centering necessitates using the designs in a way unlike the equal spacing given decorations facing upwards. Although the amounts vary, the band of space along the bottom edge will usually be larger than that at the top.

The sides of corner fillers must also conform to the lengths of the panels' edges. The delicate design in Illus. 154 is an example. There should be no doubt as to which side would be placed next to the large edge of a panel.

The narrow lines of the design are intended for chasing. Carving of this kind may be done with an incising tool or, if decorating firm wood, with a tool used in the engraving of gunstocks. A person proficient in chip carving should be able to duplicate the design and maintain proper proportions without difficulty.

The craftsman should consider spotting carvings in places besides right-angled corners. Different kinds of projections, such as handles, accept the carvings. Those having two handles may well accept duplicate designs. The placement of a filler should be not in just any open area but where the features of the product make it acceptable. The product's shape, the grain of the wood, the available surface area, and the intrinsic qualities of the design are among the factors to consider.

Illus. 155 shows a product planned to take advantage of the beneficial effect that a filler can provide. The design is simply incised and follows the general contour of the surface between the circular and ovaloid edges. The parts are unified and balanced without a connecting border. Similarities of size and shape produce the necessary unity. These features, when given the opposing positions shown, leave the viewer with the comfortable sense of the compositional balance required in a formalized arrangement.

Chamfering Edges

Chamfering produces a slope on an edge. Its form varies from a straight bevel to a complex set of undulating curves. The process of producing a chamfer by hand provides a good test of a carver's ability with flat chisels.

The purpose of chamfering is decoration, although it may have a secondary bearing on strength. Chamfers are used in architectural work instead of edge-sawing as a means of decorating without removing as much wood. Strength becomes important as the weight supported by the board or timber increases in relation to size. In ordinary applications, the superiority of the carved edge derives from the distinctive appearance of handcrafting.

A most interesting application occurs when an edge has been diversely chamfered. A pleasing effect results from cuts made at about 45°, with depth ranging from nothing to nearly the full thickness of the board. The bevel thus formed has a characteristically rhythmic curvature.

The carving of chamfers follows the usual procedure of design development, layout, and execution. The process begins by drawing the ogee on paper. Carefully sketching the lines onto the wood is the most direct approach. A few points should be marked off to help keep the curves in proportion (Illus. 156); then guidelines are drawn with a soft pencil so portions not removed when chamfering can be erased or sanded away (Illus. 157). Lines sketched on both faces at the edge will guide the removal of wood (Illus. 158–159). Sawing with a fine-toothed

Illus. 156. Edge carving begins by establishing guide points . . .

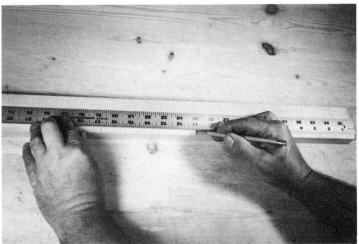

Illus. 157. Pencilling depth by hand . . .

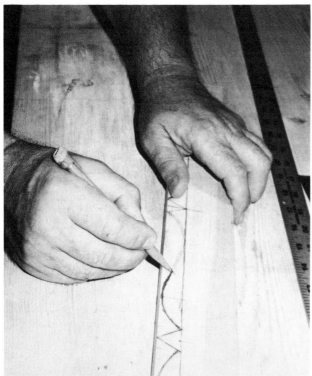

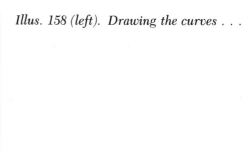
Illus. 158 (left). Drawing the curves . . .

Illus. 159 (below). Marking the adjacent edge . . .

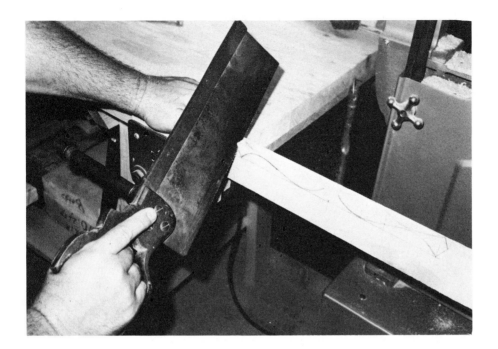

blade is done along the straight lines and in places where a cut or two will help gauge the depth for chiselling (Illus. 160). A final paring with the chisel produces a smooth finish which needs little sanding (Illus. 161–163).

Illus. 164 shows the carved pine in place as a

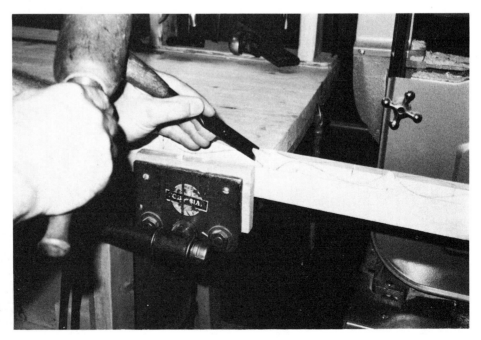

Illus. 161. Shaping with a flat chisel . . .

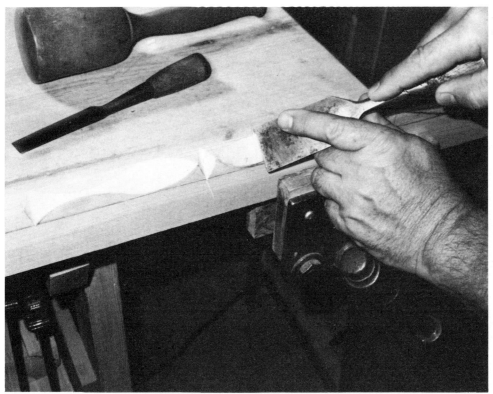

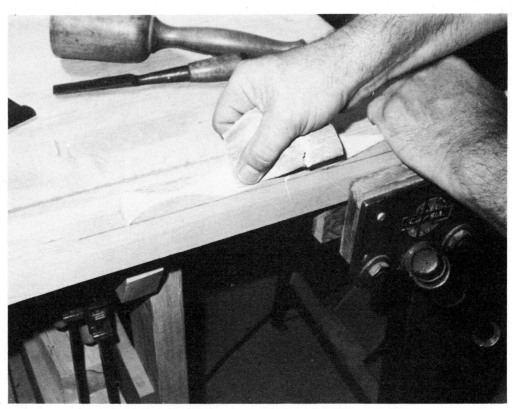

Illus. 163. And
sanding sparingly.

Illus. 164. The finished shelf support is shown here in place.

support for a closet shelf, with the chamfer in full view. Two coats of clear, durable finish protect the wood.

The ogee provides a graceful form of edge chamfering, and it can be readily altered to suit conditions of space. Portions of the curve can be readily shortened or lengthened, repeated more than twice in a row, or alternated with other compatible elements. Several of the possibilities are seen in Illus. 165. Novices may be surprised at the ease with which chisels can be controlled when duplicating the curve in wood.

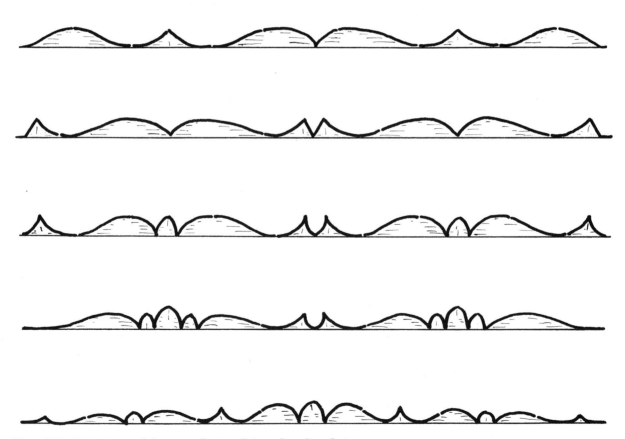

Illus. 165. Variations of the ogee designed for edge chamfering.

Carving Alternate Forms

Another form of edge design has been used in constructing the project in Illus. 166. It has been adapted from the ball-and-bead pattern which sometimes forms the borders on flat surfaces. In border applications the figures are carved to about half depth, while in these edge patterns they are given a more rounded shape. Completeness of shape, ease in carving, and functionality in gripping make the design superior as an edge carving.

Insofar as possible, the construction of the knife holder should be closely inspected as it pertains to the decoration. The length of the carved details, their use in helping to hide the joints, and the way most of the grain of the butternut remains unimbellished are all important. Possibly unnoticed are the relative lengths of the patterns on the slanted and vertical edges. The slanted details are longer so the tops and bottoms of the design align all the way around. Unless a design receives this kind of attention, the probability of the finished work being all it should is very low.

The beginning edge carver can learn by applying the designs shown, but he will want to do more of his own creating as his confidence and ability grows. Reproducing the design shown in Illus. 164 could be a worthwhile starting point. With experience, modifications and new applications will be sought. Developing and using designs in different ways makes woodcarving design an engaging process.

Regardless of the level of skill, the correct use of principles continues to be essential. The process begins with a determination of matters of fundamental importance in design—whether the article should have a center carving, a border, and edge decoration, or none of the above. A decoration must not be applied to merely any product or in just any fashion. It must be visible to be appreciated. The shelf support and the knife holder show how a design can be clearly presented. An edge carving beneath the lip of a box lid would be largely hidden.

Visibility alone, though, does not determine the placement of a design. Flat, horizontal surfaces are seldom decorated along a perimeter for reasons of appearance and the effects of handling. Thus, boxes of various sizes are ordinarily left plain along exterior edges.

Edge carvings are most suitably located along the lower extremities of boards placed with the flat vertical. Some chair rails, desk aprons, curtain valances, and shelf supports are suitable for carving. Mouldings, such as on a fireplace mantel, are another example.

Illus. 166. A suitable form of edge carving decorates this knife holder of butternut.

Using Manufactured Strips

Fortunately (or unfortunately, depending on a person's perspective) many of the mouldings now produced for architectural trim are mass produced, either machine carved or embossed under pressure. All have identifiable characteristics distinguishing them from individually carved pieces, and a discerning woodcarver will be able to make the distinction at once. Nevertheless, this doesn't make them unusable or even undesirable. They do save time.

In either building or cabinetwork, machine-produced trim works best where paint will be applied. An opaque coating will cover differences in grain, color, and surface texture. Use only the best pieces, however. Some are pathetically poor imitations.

Illus. 167. Two-plane lettering, a carved overlay, and a manufactured strip are used in this sign for a seaside establishment.

A commercially carved imitation of rope outlines the central portion of the sign in Illus. 167. The strip comes half round for ease in mounting. While the means of production is exposed at the corner, the finished border compensates somewhat for that shortcoming. The gold color brilliantly complements the blue-green of the panel, and the design appropriately supports the entire seashore motif.

Other carved portions are the result of handwork. The lettering stands out in two-plane relief from the background, which was shallowly carved. The sculptured dolphin is a half-round overlay in pine.

Manufacturing strips should be used cautiously. The one in the sign is no exception. Many of the designs are copies of hand-carvings of relatively recent origin, and many imitate originals developed in a bygone era.

Avoiding Anachronisms

The woodcarver should be acutely aware of the limitations of using copies of ornaments from early work. Some designs, like acanthus leaves and egg-and-dart patterns, are totally antiquated. They are much too dated for modern use, except where reproductions and antiques make up the decor. Only by modifying or extensively redesigning the forms can many of them become compatible with a contemporary style of decoration.

When copying designs, anachronous combinations must be avoided. Mixing designs from different periods could ruin a design completely. A Gothic door with a beautifully carved trefoil fixed to a cabinet trimmed in the colonial style is an example. Not only are the combined styles not in harmony, but the two designs carry their own particular significance.

Centuries-old designs of importance, such as the Gothic linenfold, have often retained their original meaning. In the Italian Renaissance, renewed use was made of the lotus, acanthus, scrolls, urns, and other classic ornaments of Greece and Rome. They had less of the religious association found in the Gothic carvings. Later works survived as more of a personal symbol of their designer. Chippendale's ball-and-claw design, Hepplewhite's three-feathered ostrich plume, and Duncan Phyfe's carved lyre continue today to identify the craftsmen's styles. For the uninformed woodcarver, an indiscriminate application of historical forms can lead to severely displeasing mixtures.

Considering the general practice of design in recent years, much more should be said about carving styling throughout history. Earlier styles, with ornately carved details, are less appropriate today. The same is true of the entwined foliage of Renaissance style and the classical Greek and Roman. The exceptions occur when objects are given a style which matches that of other furnishings of an historical period. The carving of a swag, a classic indeed, would also be entirely out of place with twentieth-century design. The apparent conflict is seen in Illus. 168. Other examples may be seen in some of the more poorly made articles being distributed commercially.

None of this means that designs from an earlier period must be avoided. Creating new applications from past practices continues to be an acceptable approach in design. Carved details have been, and still are, carried forward in the transition from one period to the next. Fluted and reeded carvings are familiar examples of the practice. The problem is to avoid the incongruity that results from combining features prominently associated with different periods. By and large, contemporary adaptations work best after studying the forms as they have been transmitted through time.

Illus. 168. An illustration of blatant anachronism wherein a classical design is given a place on an appliance of recent origin and style.

XI

TEXTURES
AND PATTERNS

Subject, style, and method are basic variables in woodcarving. Personal preferences and compositional qualities are also involved. Due consideration must be given the different factors, and they should be applied with the care and skill expected of a competent craftsman.

The designer has available a number of possibilities not previously covered. Surface texture, patterned arrangements, novel designs, and folk art are among them. Application of the technique should help spur new ideas

Creating Contrast

The fundamental means of creating variety by contrast is to diversify adjacent parts. Use of dissimilar sizes, shapes, textures, patterns, emotional expressions, and depths of cut helps in differentiating one thing from the next. Without adequate contrast, a composition will lack emphasis and may seem intolerably dull.

The relief carving on the lid of the trinket box in Illus. 169 has several of these distinguishing features. Its contrast comes from carving subject and background to uneven depths. The central shape and the circular leaves stand apart, and the gouge marks contrast with the smooth surfaces. An equally impressive design could be obtained with depth and texture applied in alternate ways,

Illus. 169. Texture in relief carvings can be created by tooling either the background or an object's surface.

for variations are attainable in many ways within a given series of shapes and compositions. Full realization of the alternatives gives the designer many options.

The wood used in the trivet box has a grain structure which has little natural beauty. Unlike the grainier woods, basswood lacks contrast, making some form of decoration essential. A carving serves very well, especially when given a prominent texture.

Forming Texture

The natural texture resulting from a wood's growth can be altered by the finish. The fibres may be either sanded smooth or roughly sculptured. The designer controls the blending of elements to achieve an effect appealing to both sight and touch.

Gouging, stippling, and V-tooling are three ways to produce texture. They are customarily employed in relief carvings, and are used at times on carvings in the round. Their use in forming background in relief is quite common due, in part, to the difficulty of making the bottoms of cavities smooth. Whatever the purpose, an intentionally patterned texture looks much better than unsuccessful attempts at smoothing the wood.

Illus. 170. A sample board of textures made by gouging (top), stippling (center), a V-tooling (bottom).

Textures can be created in seemingly endless form. The varieties shown in Illus. 170 suggest some possibilities. Gouging has become extremely popular, since it can be altered to suit almost any condition. Applications require a cutting tool kept sharp enough to slice across the grain. Cross-hatching with V-tools requires care in spacing, also.

Stippled patterns are ordinarily applied to carved backgrounds with specially shaped tools. Grinding the tip of a common nail to a smooth point makes an inexpensive tool. Small circles, diamonds, and triangles are easily produced shapes, while larger geometric figures can be formed on the nail's head. Manufactured tools are also available. Several of the less elaborately detailed versions sold for embossing leather offer acceptable alternatives. A word of caution: Many of the designs of these manufactured items are not appropriate for decorating woodwork of high quality.

Stippling also has a practical purpose. In addition to obscuring small defects, a sharp stippler and hammer make fine details possible when special carving tools are not available. The background in deep and acutely angled corners sometimes takes stippling more readily than sharp cutting.

Varying Surface Quality

The textural characteristics of an object are most important on carvings shaped fully in the round. Texture on sculptured pieces can simulate detail or serve as adornment. Both random and uniformly patterned arrangements are permissible. Proper staining or painting, followed by the carving of texture, leaves a highly unique and impressive result.

When carving animals, texture should be of the proper kind and be placed only where needed. Skilfully carved textures can give the effect of curly wool on a sheep, stringy hair on a goat, and the grizzly appearance of a bear. Any roughness of surface from gouging or stippling will be largely out of place if the animal has a naturally smooth skin. Very little experience is needed to know that a whale should not be cross-hatched, except in some whimsical or bizarre type of design.

A more challenging problem confronts those trying to decide how much surface detail to carve, for example, on a feathered creature. Choice of style gives a clue to the answer. The feel and appearance of real feathers will always be preferred in a naturalistic copy, while the smooth wood of a carved simulation goes with the more stylized or abstract representations. Size is important, too. The precise detailing of feathers takes on greater significance as the work approaches actual size.

The selective use of gouge marks on the stylized owl in Illus. 171 indicates somewhat of an intermediate application. The fine markings

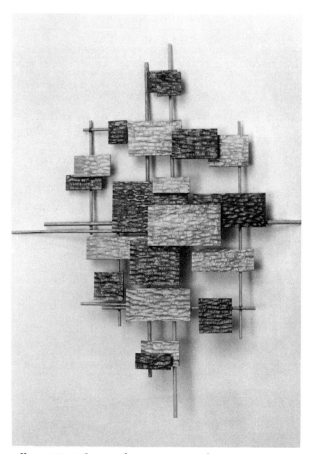

Illus. 172. The random patterns of gouge carving on the cherry and pine blocks tend to offset the starkness of this geometric assembly.

Illus. 171. Skillfully applied tool markings simulate detail and add variety to this representation of an owl carved in spruce.

on the breast, gradated into a smoothness along the wings, suggest the natural contrast between the small feathers and the sleek ones. If the breast were made smooth, the carving would be without a major area of interest.

The carving of texture is essentially decorative. Although tooled patterns seem to divert attention from smoother finishes, they should be applied so that they agree warmly with surrounding features. They must create contrast without disharmony.

Applied textures have a place in designs of all styles and in all methods of carving. An application decorates the geometric arrangement in Illus. 172. The piece derives exclusively from geometry. All aspects are decorative. The carving does nothing more than provide surface texture. Without this easily fashioned adornment, the lightness of the pine and darkness of the cherry might not provide the measure of interest intended. Considered as an entity, the assembly represents nothing more than a balanced arrangement of blocks and rods. No special meaning is suggested.

The formal elements of design in the composition weigh upon the viewer. The emphasis on mass, space, and geometric form make placement of the assembly best on a wall where the decor accepts it. As the eye would have it, the point of balanced suspension centers midway on a side-to-side viewing of the piece.

Other attractive wall decorations in the style shown can be made by modifying or completely changing certain features. Spherical segments or ovoids in place of the rectangular blocks could make a good alternative. Since space has the effect of negative mass in sculptured compositions, distance among the blocks requires variable treatment in all directions. No more than three woods should be used, and two species are sufficient for a contrast of color in the textured pieces.

Grouping Designs

Natural, geometric, and abstract subjects are adaptable to patterned arrangements, although practically any motif can be arranged in repetitive order over an area. There are few limitations. Subject, style, and arrangement are matters of personal preference.

The world about us is replete with different kinds of details in orderly distribution, and several of them have long inspired the work of woodcarvers. Geometry, too, has a definite place in this manner of decorating. Aside from chip carving, which usually involves the repetitive use of triangles by its nature, a geometric distribution underlies the grouping of designs in all patterns. The regularity of spacing gives rise to the repetition, which is frequently placed about a series of adjacent squares or diamonds. Illus. 173 shows an example.

Wallpaper and textiles commonly contain man-made, uniformly repeated designs. By studying the groupings, one will find an offset

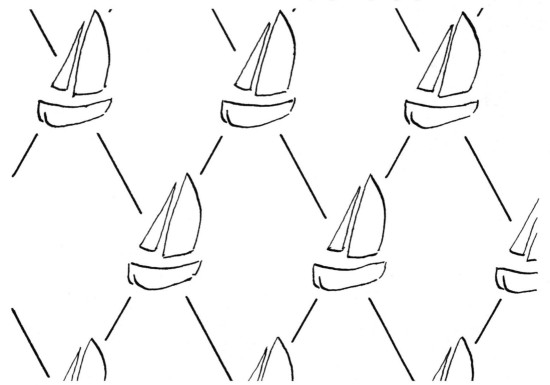

Illus. 173. Patterns repeated all over an area are customarily arranged along some form of parallelogram.

133

from one row to the next. Quarter drop, half drop, and full drop indicate several of the spacings frequently employed. No set rule governs the choice of grouping.

Along with symmetry, an arrangement must conform to the principles of design. Dominance and subordination of elements for contrast, repetition of a feature for unity, and variation of parts to overcome monotony are most important, as are the formation of lines and shapes to develop rhythm, and the provision of a transitional quality for leading the eye comfortably from part to part. Principles applicable to a solitary design generally apply to a group, though an additional one is to repeat elements at uniformly equal intervals and close enough to present a unified appearance.

Illus. 174 shows a carved application. The pattern includes a floral subject incised with a penknife and a gouge. Continuity of detail in several directions provides an element of interest.

Illus. 174. The diversified pattern on this cylindrical surface was incised with penknife and gouge.

Designing Whimsically

A whimsical woodcarving, whether done in a pattern or not, is fun for both adults and children. Small children, especially, seem to be pleasantly intrigued by baby animals with certain human characteristics. A cuddly figure with a smiling face and pants or a skirt usually gets a giggle. Adults, presumably the more sophisticated of the age groups, frequently like animals with subtle expressions such as coquettishness or vainness. The different creative slants provide considerable room for the designer's talent.

Whimsical art lacks realism. It is novel, and ranges from the fanciful to the fantastic, even to the grotesque. A whimsical subject may be both funny and out of the ordinary. A fanciful but pleasingly humorous design is generally preferred to ridiculous, absurd, or displeasingly odd ones. The woodcarver's ability to create the preferred expressions of emotion will probably determine the extent of his work in this area.

Whimsical designs do best when they avoid extraordinarily freakish art. It is one thing to put a coy smile on the face of a rabbit, but quite another to produce a horrible monster. The designer should not attempt to be too clever, either. A vegetable carved with airplane propellers attached would be both nonsensical and humorless.

Two fanciful designs are presented in Illus. 175. The stylized, unnatural qualities are apparent. Although these figures have pleasant expressions, that need not always be the case when imparting humorous characteristics to animals. They could just as easily be depicted as serious card-playing characters with dark eyeglasses, for example.

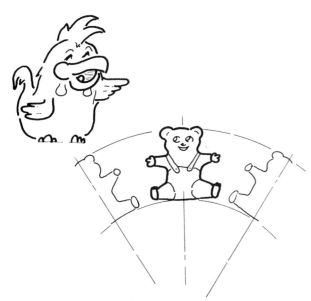

Illus. 175. Whimsical figures—these gleeful and happy—are adaptable to carvings in the round and in patterns.

Imitating Folk Art

American folk–art designs are usually identified according to a particular cultural group or, as often occurs, are referred to generically as *country*. Whether or not given a specific locality of origin, the work is very popular. Many ordinary homeowners have joined collectors who make a special habit of acquiring objects made and decorated in this manner.

Country art has several distinctly identifiable features. Flat colors are common. They give an aged effect, especially on objects of wood. Stencilling seems to be favored, as well. Even those designs brushed on unaided are spaced apart in imitation of stencilled patterns. Flowers and leaves are separated from their stems, and small sections of designs that would fit neatly into a hand-held template are repeated end on end along the corners of a room. Designs are applied similarly to small wooden articles, although they are less frequently repeated there.

Welcome companionship and love of fellow man are very apparent in country decorations. Thus, tulips and hearts are among the favorite subjects (Illus. 176.) Those figures commonly adorn the woodwork and walls in the homes of folk-art enthusiasts.

Homey mottos and welcome signs on flat pieces of wood are popular displays. Hearts, flowers, and leaves often surround the lettering. Usually, both the message and the decoration are stencilled.

Illus. 176. When making a sign from old barn siding, the layout can be easily removed if done in chalk.

When making signs, the method may have to be adapted to the wood used. For example, greeting signs made from rough wood may be more easily carved than stencilled. Weathered barn siding produces a highly desirable effect. Although a knot or two adds to the wood's rustic charm, a piece should allow easy carving. If only cupped boards are available, they can be flattened by wetting and clamping until dry.

The board may be prepared for country decorating by giving it irregular ends. The parts to be carved are then lightly outlined. Chalk is best since it can be easily removed (Illus. 177). The lettering, stems, and leaves are incised (Illus. 178); the flower heads gouged. Flat acrylics finish the article (Illus. 179). The ends of the raw wood are colored to blend with the weathered grey surface, and the flowers are given a complementary red-to-peach color. Green acrylic produces a naturalness in the stems and leaves (Illus. 180).

Certain folkcrafts, too, are indigenous to rural America, particularly the shaping of domestic animals from boards. Unless the wood has long been exposed outdoors, the flat shapes are given rounded edges and stain or paint for a weathered effect. The quaint, crude, primitive work done by some craftsmen is appealing to many collectors. Objects made of pine or maple are most preferred for their authenticity when duplicating early American crafts. Many times the objects are finished with solid paints.

Illus. 177. A country "welcome" must be incised boldly on the weathered pine board.

Illus. 178. The carved flowers and sawed ends of the board are painted with flat acrylics of appropriate colors.

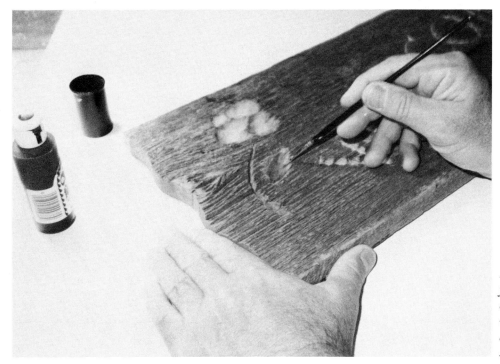

Illus. 179. No other finish should be applied to the weathered wood of an authentic country sign.

Illus. 180. American folk art often makes use of tulip, leaf, and heart motifs in border and corner decorations.

Preparing Patterns

The development of a design for woodcarving begins as a paper-and-pencil exercise, although when making more than a single carving from a design, the craftsman may find it to his advantage to do subsequent drawings directly on the wood.

Designs being prepared for the first time should almost always be sketched, and those of intricate detail should be developed in a series of sketches.

With the shape outlined to the desired size, the problem becomes a matter of transferring it to the wood. There are several methods of doing this, including tracing over carbon paper or,

137

positioning it face down on the wood and rubbing the backside. The result from rubbing will be a mirror image, a problem when transferring non-symmetrical shapes. Another method is pricking along the figure's outline with a sharp instrument; then connecting the marks made on the wood using a pencil. Blackening the paper's backside with a lead pencil before transferring is yet another idea.

The nature of the design in patterned arrangements may dictate the method chosen. Those involving a frequently repeated shape are best kept to size and spacing using a template (Illus. 181). Geometric patterns, as a rule, are often

Illus. 181. Repeated patterns are handily drawn with the aid of a template, as in this homey use of hearts for a box of keepsakes.

Illus. 182. Projects with patterns formed by chip carving are usually protected with a clear finish.

most easily drawn directly on the wood with mechanical drawing instruments. Irregular designs seem to be quite readily constructed freehand after locating a few points by measuring.

When the size of a pattern must be changed, the person who has little confidence in his ability to draw freehand might consider using a mechanical method of enlargement or reduction. Proportional dividers, proportionally drawn squares, offset measurements from right-angled edges, and lines extending from a point through selected places on the design's outline are all valid methods. Each provides a means of locating points to be connected when re-creating individual shapes.

For shapes repeated in a series, more direct methods are better. Photo copiers will now reproduce designs in almost any size normally wanted. A pantograph is another option. This instrument has four bars forming a parallelogram with an aligned pivot, tracer, and marking point. The choice between the two may depend on availability.

Finishing Woodcarvings

Finishing is necessary. Bare wood collects dust, and oil from handling eventually leads to its discoloration. Water could also mar the wood. It not only leaves permanent stains, it raises the grain. With time and no protection, unfinished wood can dry out, crack, and warp. A fine woodcarving could be ruined.

While a finish can beautify, it can also detract from the art work. The results depends on the type of finish and its application. Often approached with trepidation, the finishing of well made carvings seems to be more difficult for some than it need be. Commercially packaged finishes come with clear directions which, when followed, will lead to quality results (Illus. 182).

A clear finish of lacquer, varnish, or oil is preferred by some woodcarvers. These materials seal the wood without hiding the grain. Artist's paint (oils or acrylics) are used at times for tinting, spotting, or completely covering the wood. Stain also can be used to make a carving stand out.

Oil penetrates the pores of the wood. It is easy to apply, leaves a low lustre, but does not do much to protect from abrasion. Lacquer finishes protect the surface well, but they are somewhat difficult to apply by brushing. Subsequent coats dissolve the previous ones. Varnish, also a surface finish, has lately become quite easy to apply. On woodcarvings, it should be brushed on carefully in thin coats to avoid running or build-up.

Generally, water-based finishes should *not* be used on woodcarvings, because they tend to raise the grain. Oil-based stains are preferred. Acrylic paint, a water-solvent material, imparts a realistic color and can be controlled best by first applying a thin sealer coat of polyurethane. The wet acrylics can then be wiped thin for a translucent effect. An application of wax makes a good final coat, but the dullness of weathered surfaces and the flatness of acrylic paints are preferable for country creations.

A decision about artificial color on a woodcarv-

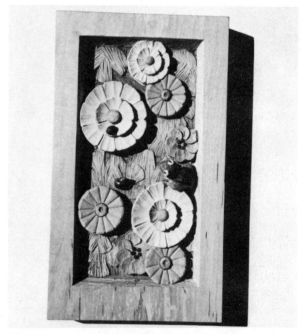

Illus. 183. Unity of composition and contrast of detail in this stylization of pond life are strengthened by the selective use of color on the floral patterns.

ing may depend on the appearance of the wood and the nature of the subject. The plainness of grain and dullness of color of some woods are indicators, but the message or idea the wood-carver hopes to convey may be the major deciding factor. Illus. 183 shows a buckeye creation in which those considerations were taken fully into account. Unquestionably, the different hues impart a sense of dynamism which otherwise would not be entirely present.

The craftsman should not hesitate to experiment with new finishes as they come on the market. Nontoxic, water-resistant, and long-wearing qualities are continually being improved. Polyurethane is a good example.

A type of varnish, polyurethane makes an excellent clear finish. It is durable, and it effectively enhances a piece with a dull or satin sheen. The formulations for exterior use work well on signs and utilitarian pieces subjected to washing. A single coat also makes a good sealant on woodcarvings colored with acrylics.

GLOSSARY

Abstract. A style characterized either by little or no reference to the appearance of objects in nature.

Aesthetic. Pertaining to beauty in fine art.

Anachronism. Anything incongruous in point of time, as in mixing designs of different period styles.

Asymmetrical. Lack of formal symmetry, especially bilateral symmetry, between parts of a design.

Balance. Physical or visual equilibrium of the elements in a design, such as mass and color.

Caricature. A subject represented by exaggeration or distortion of characteristics.

Chroma. Any color having hue, as distinguished from white, black, and grey.

Contrast. Diversity of adjacent parts as opposed to gradation of color, transition in shape, or harmony of elements.

Conventionalized. A style in accord with general custom, accepted practice, or rule of art in which repetition and formal arrangement are customary.

Diaper. A pattern of repeated unity such that the outline of one element forms part of the adjacent elements.

Embellish. To adorn, decorate, or enrich with detail.

Folk art. Paintings, sculpture, etc., produced in country manner.

Form. The contour or shape of an object.

Formalism. Predominant attention to arranging according to conventional or traditional rules.

Geometric. A style utilizing lines, planes, patterns, and other shapes having basis in geometry.

Harmony. Agreement among parts of a design, thereby producing unity of effect and a pleasing whole.

Idealism. The pursuit of perfection by showing things as they are desired to be instead of as they are.

Mass. Matter concentrated as a single body or that portion of a work distinguished by unified color, shading, texture, etc.

Motif. The central idea, theme, or dominant feature of a work.

Naturalistic. Reproducing items as they appear in nature.

Objective design. The thing, tangible or intangible, towards which a composition is consciously directed.

Ovoid. Egg-shaped and similar to oval.

Proportion. Relative size, ratio, magnitude, or degree and disposition of arrangement.

Realistic. A style typified by close correspondence between a representation and the thing itself.

Rhythm. The regular, often flowing recurrence of similar features in a composition.

Rococo. Any overelaborate decoration of massed-together details.

Stylized. A style having a distinctive mode of expression apart from the duplication of nature.

Subjective design. A work making prominent the individuality of the designer—his or her views, emotions, and expressions.

Symbolic. Pertaining to a representative sign or emblem, as the dove is symbolic of peace and digits represent numbers.

Symmetry. Balance between halves of an arrangement or single object.

Unity. The ordering of parts so as to constitute a whole and undivided effect.

Utilitarian. Consisting of a practical, rather than a spiritual, usefulness.

INDEX